S E R I E S

A NavPress Bible study on the book of

1 PETER

A MINISTRY OF THE NAVIGATORS
P.O. BOX 35001, COLORADO SPRINGS, COLORADO 80935

The Navigators is an international Christian
organization. Our mission is to reach, disciple, and
equip people to know Christ and to make Him known
through successive generations. We envision multi-
tudes of diverse people in the United States and every
other nation who have a passionate love for Christ,
live a lifestyle of sharing Christ's love, and multiply
spiritual laborers among those without Christ.

NavPress is the publishing ministry of The Navigators.
NavPress publications help believers learn biblical
truth and apply what they learn to their lives and min-
istries. Our mission is to stimulate spiritual formation
among our readers.

Printed in the United States of America

16 17 18 19 20 / 99 98

CONTENTS

ACKNOWLEDGMENTS

The LIFECHANGE series has been produced through the coordinated efforts of a team of Navigator Bible study developers and NavPress editorial staff, along with a nationwide network of fieldtesters.

SERIES EDITOR: KAREN LEE-THORP

HOW TO USE THIS STUDY

Objectives

Each guide in the LIFECHANGE series of Bible studies covers one book of the Bible. Although the LIFECHANGE guides vary with the individual books they explore, they share some common goals:

1. To provide you with a firm foundation of understanding and a thirst to return to the book;
2. To teach you by example how to study a book of the Bible without structured guides;
3. To give you all the historical background, word definitions, and explanatory notes you need, so that your only other reference is the Bible;
4. To help you grasp the message of the book as a whole;
5. To teach you how to let God's Word transform you into Christ's image.

Each lesson in this study is designed to take 60 to 90 minutes to complete on your own. The guide is based on the assumption that you are completing one lesson per week, but if time is limited you can do half a lesson per week or whatever amount allows you to be thorough.

Flexibility

LIFECHANGE guides are flexible, allowing you to adjust the quantity and depth of your study to meet your individual needs. The guide offers many optional questions in addition to the regular numbered questions. The optional questions, which appear in the margins of the study pages, include the following:

Optional Application. Nearly all application questions are optional; we hope you will do as many as you can without overcommitting yourself.

For Thought and Discussion. Beginning Bible students should be able to handle these, but even advanced students need to think about them. These questions frequently deal with ethical issues and other biblical principles. They often offer cross-references to spark thought, but the references do not give

5

obvious answers. They are good for group discussions.

For Further Study. These include: a) cross-references that shed light on a topic the book discusses, and b) questions that delve deeper into the passage. You can omit them to shorten a lesson without missing a major point of the passage.

(Note: At the end of lessons two through twelve you are given the option of outlining the passage just studied. Although the outline is optional, you will almost surely find it worthwhile.)

If you are meeting in a group, decide together which optional questions to prepare for each lesson, and how much of the lesson you will cover at the next meeting. Normally, the group leader should make this decision, but you might let each member choose his own application questions.

As you grow in your walk with God, you will find the LIFECHANGE guide growing with you—a helpful reference on a topic, a continuing challenge for application, a source of questions for many levels of growth.

Overview and Details

The guide begins with an overview of the book. The key to interpretation is context—what is the whole passage or book *about*?—and the key to context is purpose—what is the author's *aim* for the whole work? In lesson one you will lay the foundation for your study by asking yourself, Why did the author (and God) write the book? What did they want to accomplish? What is the book about?

Then, in lesson two, you will begin analyzing successive passages in detail. Thinking about how a paragraph fits into the overall goal of the book will help you to see its purpose. Its purpose will help you see its meaning. Frequently reviewing a chart or outline of the book will enable you to make these connections.

Finally, in the last lesson, you will review the whole book, returning to the big picture to see whether your view of it has changed after closer study. Review will also strengthen your grasp of major issues and give you an idea of how you have grown from your study.

Kinds of Questions

Bible study on your own—without a structured guide—follows a progression. First you observe: What does the passage *say*? Then you interpret: What does the passage *mean*? Lastly you apply: How does this truth affect my life?

Some of the "how" and "why" questions will take some creative thinking, even prayer, to answer. Some are opinion questions without clearcut right answers; these will lend themselves to discussions and side studies.

Don't let your study become an exercise of knowledge alone. Treat the passage as God's Word, and stay in dialogue with Him as you study. Pray, "Lord, what do you want me to see here?" "Father, why is this true?" "Lord, how does this apply to my life?"

It is important that you write down your answers. The act of writing clarifies your thinking and helps you to remember.

Meditating on verses is an option in several lessons. Its purpose is to let biblical truth sink into your inner convictions so that you will increasingly be able to act on this truth as a natural way of life. You may want to find a quiet place to spend five minutes each day repeating the verse(s) to yourself. Think about what each word, phrase, and sentence means to you. During the rest of the day, remind yourself of the verse(s) at intervals.

Study Aids

A list of reference materials, including a few notes of explanation to help you make good use of them, begins on page 133. This guide is designed to include enough background to let you interpret with just your Bible and the guide. Still, if you want more information on a subject or want to study a book on your own, try the references listed.

Scripture Versions

Unless otherwise indicated, the Bible quotations in this guide are from the New International Version of the Bible. Other versions cited are the Revised Standard Version (RSV), the New American Standard Bible (NASB), and the King James Version (KJV).

Use any translation you like for study, preferably more than one. A paraphrase such as The Living Bible is not accurate enough for study, but it can be helpful for comparison or devotional reading.

Memorizing and Meditating

A Psalmist wrote, "I have hidden your word in my heart that I might not sin against you" (Psalm 119:11). If you write down a verse or passage that challenges or encourages you, and reflect on it often for a week or more, you will find it beginning to affect your motives and actions. We forget quickly what we read once; we remember what we ponder.

When you find a significant verse or passage, you might copy it onto a card to keep with you. Set aside five minutes during each day just to think about what the passage might mean in your life. Recite it over to yourself, exploring its meaning. Then, return to your passage as often as you can during your day, for a brief review. You will soon find it coming to mind spontaneously.

For Group Study

A group of four to ten people allows the richest discussions, but you can adapt this guide for other sized groups. It will suit a wide range of group types, such as home Bible studies, growth groups, youth groups, and businessmen's studies.

Both new and experienced Bible students, new and mature Christians, will benefit from the guide. You can omit or leave for later years any questions you find too easy or too hard.

The guide is intended to lead a group through one lesson per week. However, feel free to split lessons if you want to discuss them more thoroughly. Or, omit some questions in a lesson if preparation or discussion time is limited. You can always return to this guide for personal study later on. You will be able to discuss only a few questions at length, so choose some for discussion and others for background. Make time at each discussion for members to ask about anything that gave them trouble.

Each lesson in the guide ends with a section called *For the Group.* These sections give advice on how to focus a discussion, how you might apply the lesson in your group, how you might shorten a lesson, and so on. The group leader should read each *For the Group* at least a week ahead so that he or she can tell the group how to prepare for the next lesson.

Each member should prepare for a meeting by writing answers for all the background and discussion questions to be covered. If the group decides not to take an hour per week for private preparation, then expect to take at least two meetings per lesson to work through the questions. Application will be very difficult, however, without private thought and prayer.

Two reasons for studying in a group are accountability and support. When each member commits in front of the rest to seek growth in an area of life, you can pray with one another, listen jointly for God's guidance, help one another to resist temptation, assure each other that the other's growth matters to you, use the group to practice spiritual principles, and so on. Pray about one another's commitments and needs at most meetings. Spend the first few minutes of each meeting sharing any results from applications prompted by previous lessons. Then discuss new applications toward the end of the meeting. Follow such sharing with prayer for these and other needs.

If you write down each other's applications and prayer requests, you are more likely to remember to pray for them during the week, ask about them next meeting, and notice answered prayers. You might want to get a notebook for prayer requests and discussion notes.

Notes taken during discussion will help you to remember, follow up on ideas, stay on the subject, and clarify a total view of an issue. But don't let note-taking keep you from participating. Some groups choose one member at each meeting to take notes. Then someone copies the notes and distributes them at the next meeting. Rotating these tasks can help include people. Some groups have someone take notes on a large pad of paper or erasable marker board (pre-formed shower wallboard works well), so that everyone can see what has been recorded.

Page 136 lists some good sources of counsel for leading group studies. The *Small Group Letter,* published by NavPress, is unique, offering insights from experienced leaders every other month.

BACKGROUND

Peter and His Readers

Map of the Roman Empire

Simon Peter

Simon was a common name, the Greek version of the Hebrew name *Simeon* (Acts 15:14). Simon was born in Bethsaida (John 1:44), near the north shore of the Sea of Galilee. His family were Jewish fishermen, like many of their neighbors, although many Samaritans and Greek-speaking Gentiles also lived in Galilee. Simon probably received "the normal elementary education of a Jewish boy in a small town"[1]—that is, he learned to read a little Hebrew and enough Greek to do business, and he spoke Aramaic and common Greek flu-

9

ently. He was not trained in the Jewish Scriptures and law as a rabbi, nor in literary Greek (Acts 4:13). Before meeting Jesus, Simon may have followed John the Baptist (John 1:35-42).

Simon was one of Jesus' first and closest disciples. He was always listed first among them (Matthew 10:2-4; Luke 6:12-16, 9:28; Acts 1:13), and he may have been their leader (Luke 22:31-32). Jesus renamed him *Cephas* (Aramaic), or *Peter* (Greek), which means a pebble, a small rock. This name suggested Peter's future strength, endurance, and foundational position in the Church, and his dependence on the Church's true Rock: Jesus (Matthew 16:16-18, Ephesians 2:19-20, 1 Peter 2:4-8).

Peter the Pillar

Peter seems to have remained the leader of the apostles after Jesus' death (Acts 1:15-26), although he was leader among equals (Acts 15:13-22). The first twelve chapters of the book of Acts show Peter leading the disciples' proclamation of the risen Christ. Paul called Peter a "pillar" of the Jerusalem church during this period, from about 33-47 AD (Galatians 2:9).[2]

Paul and Peter agreed at one point that Paul would evangelize Gentiles and Peter would evangelize Jews (Galatians 2:7). But Peter did preach to Gentiles in Caesarea (Acts 10:1-11:18). We don't know what Peter did after 47 AD, but 1 Peter suggests that he worked in Asia Minor at some point.

Martyrdom

Early sources say that Peter spent the last years of his life in Rome. In 64 AD a fire broke out in Rome, destroying much of the city. Many people suspected that Emperor Nero had ordered the city burnt, so that he could rebuild it in modern style. Nero found scapegoats in an unpopular religious sect—the Christians—who were social outcasts and already suspected of wicked practices. As the Roman historian Tacitus wrote some fifty years later, "a huge crowd was convicted not so much of arson as of hatred of the human race."[3] They were executed horribly.

Although the disgusting executions made many Romans feel sorry for the Christians, the spectacle encouraged others to harass the sect. According to early Christian sources, both Peter and Paul were executed within a few years of the fire in Rome. A third-century Christian, Origen, records that Peter was crucified upside down, feeling unworthy to die as Christ had died.

Asia Minor

First Peter 1:1 says that the letter was addressed to Christians in Pontus, Galatia, Cappadocia, Asia, and Bithynia. These were Roman provinces in what is now called Asia Minor, or Turkey (see the map on page 9). Paul had founded churches in Asia and Galatia; we have letters from him to Ephesus,

Colossae, and Galatia. But Peter seems to have known these Christians as well.

By 60 AD, the churches in Asia Minor were probably converting many Gentiles and few Jews. There is some disagreement, but many scholars believe that Peter was speaking to all the Christians in the region he addressed, Jews and Gentiles, and especially newer converts.[4] He called his readers by terms that originally Jews had given themselves (1 Peter 1:1, 2:5, 2:9), but he spoke of the Christians' formerly depraved lives in terms that Jews customarily used for Gentiles (4:3). He seems to have regarded all Christians as pagans at heart before conversion, but all the true Israel after conversion.

We believe that 1 Peter was written sometime after 60 AD, probably from Rome.[5] If Peter wrote after the Roman fire, then his readers would have known of the persecution there. However, official investigations and executions were not held outside the capital city. The persecution in Asia Minor was unofficial (see the box, "Persecution in the Roman Empire," on pages 46-47).

We don't know just what prompted the great apostle to send this letter to distant Asia Minor. As you read 1 Peter, try to put yourself in the place of its first readers, and think about what Peter seems to have wanted to accomplish with this letter.

1. Irving L. Jensen, *1 and 2 Peter* (Chicago: The Moody Bible Institute, 1971), page 4.
2. Jensen, pages 7-8.
3. Tacitus, *Annals*, xv, 44.5 in F.F. Bruce, *New Testament History* (Garden City, New York: Doubleday and Company, Inc., 1971), page 401; for more, see "How Pagans Viewed Christians" on page 96 of this study guide.
4. J. N. D. Kelly, *A Commentary on the Epistles of Peter and Jude* (Grand Rapids, Michigan: Baker Book House, 1981[1969]), page 4. See also Jensen, pages 13-14, and Kenneth S. Wuest, *First Peter in the Greek New Testament* (Grand Rapids, Michigan: William B. Eerdmans Publishing Company, 1942), page 14.
5. Alan M. Stibbs, *The First Epistle General of Peter* (Grand Rapids, Michigan: William B. Eerdmans Publishing Company, 1983 [1959]), pages 64-67; Kelly, pages 218-219. See also Jensen, page 14, and Wuest, pages 132-133.

OVERVIEW

If you belonged to the cult of Isis in the first century AD, your neighbors probably would not have bothered you. And if they had bothered you, another Isis worshiper two thousand miles away would not have written to you about your troubles. The idea of being one Body, one Church, was unknown in paganism. As you read Peter's letter, try to imagine how you would have felt to receive it from the chief apostle in faraway Rome.

This overview asks you to read 1 Peter several times. Try to read it as you would approach a letter to yourself, not stopping to wrestle with individual phrases, but looking for the overall message. One reading should take an average reader about half an hour; if you don't think you are an average reader, you might try to read the letter just once or plan extra time. But even if you are "average," this may well be the most time-consuming lesson of your study. Don't get discouraged; just try to plan your time and do as much as you can. You can always return for a more thorough overview when you study 1 Peter again in a later year.

First impressions

1. Read Peter's letter at least once in one sitting, so that you can see it as a whole. You may want to read it again in another translation. Try reading parts of it aloud. Get a general impression.

2. Describe the *mood* (tone, emotion) of the letter. In other words, what seem to be Peter's attitudes or feelings toward his readers and toward his subject matter? (Is Peter formal, intimate, angry, joyful . . . ?) If you think the mood changes anywhere, note where and how it changes.

_____

_____

_____

_____

_____

3. Think about what Peter says and how he says it. How would you describe his *style*? (For instance, is he writing a story, personal news, a sermon . . . ? Is he trying to teach doctrine, urge people to act on something, encourage, rebuke, convince . . . ?)

_____

_____

_____

_____

4. *Repetition* is a key to the ideas a writer considers most important. What words or phrases occur over and over?

_____

_____

_____

_____

_____

14

As you study 1 Peter in more depth, you may notice repetition or other general impressions that you overlooked on your first reading. If you like, you can come back to this lesson to write down what you notice for future reference.

Broad outline

If your impression of 1 Peter is vague after one reading, a broad outline can help sharpen it.

5. Reread the letter, preferably in a different translation if you have read it only once so far. (A different version can help you notice new things and can make a confusing passage clearer.) This time, think of a short phrase or sentence that can serve as a title for each paragraph. It may help you to include key words from the paragraph. Write your title below. (There is no one right answer; the first title is given as an example. Your Bible's paragraph divisions may differ, so feel free to alter those given here.)

1:1-2 _Apostle to Strangers_

1:3-12 _____

1:13-21 _____

1:22-25 _____

2:1-3 _____

2:4-10 _____

2:11-12 _____

For Further Study:
Try to grasp the overall thread of Peter's discourse by grouping some of its paragraphs together. Give titles to the following sections: 1:3-2:10, 2:11-4:11 (or 2:11-3:7, 3:8-4:11), 4:12-5:14.

2:13-17 _____

_____

2:18-25 _____

_____

3:1-7 _____

_____

3:8-12 _____

_____

3:13-17 _____

_____

3:18-22 _____

_____

4:1-6 _____

_____

4:7-11 _____

_____

4:12-19 _____

_____

5:1-4 _____

_____

5:5-7 _____

_____

5:8-9 _____

_____

5:10-11 _____

_____

5:12-14 _____

Theme/purpose

People usually write letters in response to a particular situation in their own or their readers' lives. They normally have reasons for choosing the topics they cover in their letters. It is often not possible to reconstruct exactly what needs occasioned a letter, but the more we can reconstruct, the better we will understand the writer's message.

Our own purpose for studying the letter will often differ from its original purpose, but how we understand and apply a writer's words should be influenced by how he and the Holy Spirit *meant* them to be understood and applied in the first century.

6. In 5:12 Peter tells why he wrote this letter. He says he is "encouraging" (NASB: "exhorting") them to *do* some things and "testifying" that they might *believe* some things. In one sentence each, summarize what you think Peter wants his readers to believe and do. Take the whole letter into account.

believe _____

_____

_____

_____

do _____

_____

_____

_____

7. What seems to be the main theme or themes of Peter's letter? (Repeated and other important words may help here. You may also want to look for key verses.)

_____

_____

_____

For Thought and Discussion: What do you think is the relationship between doing and believing in Peter's letter?

17

_____

_____

_____

8. If you have not already done so, read the historical background on pages 9-12. If you feel that additional background information would help you to better interpret Peter's letter, you might

18

write down your questions here. Some of your questions may be answered later in this study guide. The sources on pages 133-137 may help you answer others.

_____

_____

_____

_____

_____

9. In your first readings of 1 Peter, you may have come across concepts you'd like clarified or questions you'd like answered as you go deeper into this study. While your thoughts are still fresh, you may want to jot down your questions here to serve as personal objectives for your investigation of this letter.

_____

_____

_____

_____

_____

_____

Study Skill—Application

The last step of Bible study is asking yourself, "What difference should this passage make in my life? How should it make me want to think or act?" Application will require time, thought, prayer, and perhaps even discussion with another person. You may find it more productive to concentrate on one specific application, giving it careful thought and prayer, than to list several potential applications without really reflecting on them or committing yourself to them. One step actually taken is more important than many steps supported only by good intentions!

10. Does any discovery from your first readings of 1 Peter encourage you in your current situation? If so, write down this discovery, along with any implications it has for the way you approach life. If you plan to do anything in response—such as pray, talk to someone, begin a habit, or whatever—you might write down what you plan to do.

_____

_____

_____

_____

_____

_____

_____

_____

For the group

The beginning of a new study is a good time to lay a foundation for honest sharing of ideas, for getting comfortable with each other, and for encouraging a sense of common purpose. One way to establish common ground is to talk about what each group member hopes to get out of your group—out of your study of 1 Peter, and out of any prayer, singing, sharing, service, outreach, or anything else you might do together. You could take about fifteen minutes at the beginning of your meeting to give each person a chance to share his or her vision for the group. If you have someone write down each member's hopes and expectations, then you can look back at these goals later to see if they are being met.

After that, you might approach your overview like this:

First impressions of the book (questions 1-4)— 10 minutes
Outline (question 5)—5 minutes

Themes and goals (questions 6-7)—10 minutes
Group members' questions (questions 8-9)—5
    minutes
Examples of how you might apply something
    in 1 Peter to yourselves (for members who
    are less familiar with doing
    this)—10 minutes

Don't feel you must follow this structure or its
time allotments rigidly; it is just a model for how to
go about structuring a discussion. Also, be aware
that some people are better than others at outlining,
seeing themes, and so on. Some people are better at
close analysis of a verse, or at seeing how a scripture
applies to their lives. Give thanks for each other's
strengths, and don't be embarrassed to give and
request help.

Chart of 1 Peter

Purpose: To encourage his readers to live holy lives in the midst of suffering because of their identity and hope in Christ.

1:1-2	Peter greets the "strangers."
1:3-12	Peter praises God for the strangers' hope, which gives them joy despite trials.
1:13-2:3	Peter exhorts his readers to grow in holiness and love because of their hope.
2:4-10	Peter describes the identity and purpose of his readers—a temple and priesthood made to worship God.
2:11-12	Peter urges the strangers to set godly examples for unbelievers.
2:13-17	Peter urges submission to governors as part of the godly example.
2:18-25	Peter urges submission to masters as part of the godly example and in imitation of Christ.
3:1-6	Peter urges wives to submit as part of the godly example.
3:7	Peter urges husbands to respect and be considerate as part of the godly example.
3:8-12	Peter urges all to seek harmony and so be blessed.
3:13-22	Peter urges all to face ill-treatment in light of Christ's work.
4:1-6	Peter urges his readers to abandon sin in light of Christ's work.
4:7-11	Peter urges godly community life in light of the coming end.
4:12-19	Peter urges joy in suffering for Christ.
5:1-4	Peter urges elders to lead as suits their hope.
5:5-7	Peter urges each reader to live humbly to obtain God's grace.
5:8-11	Peter urges all to resist evil in God's strength.
5:12-14	Peter summarizes his encouragement.

LESSON TWO

1 PETER 1:1-12

Praise

Sometimes we just need to know that there are reasons for what we're going through and hope beyond
it. Focusing on that knowledge can give us the
strength to persevere.

Ask God to teach you as you study 1:1-12. Then
read the passage carefully. Compare your titles of
the two paragraphs (page 15) to the subtitles in this
lesson.

The Christian's Identity (1:1-2)

In his greeting, Peter identified himself in one
phrase and his readers in two verses.

> **Study Skill—Observation**
> When you study the Bible without a study
> guide, your first step will be to make observa-
> tions and write them down. After listing every-
> thing you observe, even things that seem triv-
> ial, you will begin asking yourself who, what,
> when, where, how, and why questions like
> those in this guide.

Apostle (verse 1). Literally, "one who is sent"—a
   messenger, proxy, ambassador. In Jewish law,
   this was the *shaliach*, "a person acting with full
   authority for another."[1]

23

The early Church recognized certain men who had seen the risen Jesus as apostles—the leaders with highest authority regarding doctrine and policy. (See John 21:15-19, Acts 1:1-8, Acts 6:1-6.)

1. Note everything you observe in 1:1-2 that describes the Christian's identity.

_____

_____

_____

_____

_____

_____

Strangers . . . scattered . . . chosen (verses 1-2). These were words that Jews who lived outside Palestine used to describe themselves. They were "strangers" and "scattered" (Greek: *diaspora*) because of their exile from the land of Israel. They were "chosen" as inheritors of God's covenant.

Sanctifying (verse 2). To sanctify is to make holy, to set wholly apart for God's use. When used of people, sanctification often means the process by which the Holy Spirit transforms us into people worthy to live with the Holy God (Leviticus 11:45, 2 Corinthians 7:1, 2 Timothy 2:21, 1 Peter 1:16). But in 1 Peter 1:2, sanctification is a completed work in the believer—God has set him apart to become holy (Hebrews 10:10).[2]

Study Skill—Connecting Words
Connecting words—such as *according to, by, for, therefore, in order that, if . . . then, however,* and *but*—are clues to how statements relate to each other.

Sprinkling (verse 2). Peter's image is from Exodus 24:4-8, the ritual by which the Israelites cemented their covenant with God. The blood of bulls was sprinkled on the people to signify that they were renouncing pagan ways and that God was cleansing them from guilt to be holy.[3]

Optional Application: Meditate for five or ten minutes on what Christ's blood does for us.

2. Choose one thing Peter says in 1:1-2 about our identity as Christians, and consider it for a while. How do you think this fact should affect a Christian's attitudes and behavior?

_____

_____

_____

_____

_____

_____

_____

_____

Grace (verse 2). God's unmerited favor to humanity. It can mean the gift of blotting out our sins through Christ, but here Peter probably means "the enabling grace for daily Christian living which is given to the saint yielded to and dependent upon the Holy Spirit."[4]

Peace (verse 2). Peace is a trait of the Messianic Age (the reign of the Messiah, or Christ) foretold by the prophets. It means wholeness and well-being in all creation—man and nature flourishing and perfect. Thus, to wish someone "peace" is to wish him God's presence, and the personal fulfillment, completeness, and wholeness that flow from that presence. This is wholeness in all aspects of life—physical, psychological, social, political, and so on.[5]

Living hope (1:3-5)

Pagan and Jewish writers often began letters with
thanks for the reader's welfare and prayer that it
might continue. The formula "Praise be" (NASB, RSV:
"Blessed be") was traditional in Jewish worship (see
Luke 1:68).[6] Notice how Peter turns this traditional
opening to a Christian use.

3. Praise is making statements about who someone is and what he has done in order to honor
   him. List the character traits and actions for
   which Peter praised God in 1:3-5.

   _____

   _____

   _____

   _____

   _____

   _____

Study Skill—Cross-references
Other passages of Scripture can often shed
light on what you are studying. These are
called *cross-references*.

---

4. Peter said that Christians have been given "new
   birth into a living hope" (1:3). What do you
   learn from the following cross-references about
   that new birth?

   John 1:12-13 _____

   _____

   _____

   _____

   John 3:3-6 _____

   _____

   _____

26

Galatians 4:4-7 _____

_____

_____

_____

Optional Application: Take time to reflect on your new birth into a living hope. What does this imply for your approach to life?

Hope (1 Peter 1:3). Not a mood of wishfulness (a feeling inside you), but the content of a sure expectation (the thing you are expecting).

5. Think about the "living hope" (verse 3) that Jesus' resurrection has made available to us. In the following cross-references, note what your hope (sure expectation) is.

Romans 8:22-25 _____

_____

_____

_____

1 Corinthians 15:19-26 _____

_____

_____

_____

1 John 3:1-3 _____

_____

_____

_____

Study Skill—Paraphrasing
Paraphrasing—putting a passage of Scripture into your own words—can help you think about what each phrase in the passage means.

For Further Study:
Our inheritance
(1 Peter 1:4) is a rich
biblical theme. You
can find other refer-
ences by using a con-
cordance to find
words like *heirs,
adoption,* and *inheri-
tance.* You might be-
gin with Mark 10:17;
Romans 8:17;
1 Peter 3:7,9; or
Revelation 21:1-22:9.

**Optional
Application:** How
might what you
learned about your
hope or inheritance in
questions 4-7 affect
your current priorities
in life?

6. Summarize in your own words what you think "new birth into a living hope" means.

_____

_____

_____

_____

_____

_____

_____

7. Peter uses three words in 1 Peter 1:4 to contrast our inheritance with all other goals, desires, or treasures. Think about what you desire or treasure. Which of those things will "perish, spoil, or fade"?

_____

_____

_____

_____

_____

_____

_____

Salvation (verses 5,9-10). Peter speaks of it as a future event. In this sense, salvation means a person's deliverance from God's wrath on the Day of Judgment. It also means the total remaking of the world.

As a past event, salvation means deliverance from 1) the control of sin that kept us from being able to please God, and 2) the isolation from God caused by our sin (Colossians 1:21-23).[7]

Joy amid trials (1:6-9)

Rejoice, joy (verses 6,8). "Pleasurable emotion due to well-being or satisfaction."[8] A Christian's joy wells up from a sense that his deepest needs are met permanently. He is loved unconditionally, he has purpose, and his ongoing life is secure. Therefore, his sense of well-being does not depend upon current circumstances.[9]

8. a. We should respond to the gifts of verses 3-5 "with an inexpressible and glorious joy" (verses 6-9). But verse 6 explains why we sometimes fail to respond to God's generosity in this way. Why are we sometimes not joyful?

_____

_____

_____

_____

b. Compare 1 Peter 1:7 to James 1:2-4, and give two reasons why God permits Christians to face troubles.

_____

_____

_____

_____

_____

c. In light of these facts, why can a Christian be joyful in adversity (1 Peter 1:6-9)?

_____

_____

_____

Optional Application: Think of some challenge you are facing. Specifically how do verses 6-9 apply to this stressful situation?

_____

_____

_____

Study Skill—Keeping Lists

A list or chart can often help you to organize teaching on a theme.

Joy is the first response to suffering Peter urges upon his readers. As you continue to study his letter, notice other responses he urges (exhortations) and the reasons he gives for each (doctrine, logic). On a separate sheet of paper, or on one of the blank pages at the end of this study guide, you could keep a chart like this:

verses	responses to suffering	reasons
1:6-9	joy	

Souls (verse 9). Greeks believed that the soul was the immortal part of a person which lived in his mortal body. The soul was rational and good; the body was irrational and evil. Jews like Peter believed that when God breathed life into matter it became a "soul," a living being (Genesis 2:7). Mind and body were one living being, all good. Sin corrupted mind and body equally. (See the word _soul_ or _life_ in Luke 9:24-25; 12:15,19,20,22,23. See also 1 Corinthians 15:35-49 and Philippians 3:20-21.)[10]

Prophets and angels (1:10-12)

9. What did the Old Testament prophets and the angels long to understand before Christ came (1 Peter 1:10-12)?

_____

_____

_____

_____

_____

For Further Study:
Why do you think hearing about the longings of the prophets and angels would have encouraged Peter's readers?

10. Review what you have learned from 1:1-12. Does any discovery from this passage seem to apply to your life right now? Does some insight encourage you, or challenge you to act? If so, write down what seems important to you from this passage, along with any practical implications it might have for how you should approach your current situation. (You might reread the application Study Skill on page 19.)

_____

_____

_____

_____

_____

_____

_____

Study Skill—Memorizing and Meditating
Read the paragraph on memorizing and meditating on page 7. If there is a sentence or paragraph in 1 Peter 1:1-12 that you want to take to heart, you might copy it down and set aside time each day for the next week to meditate on it. Don't worry that you will be studying 1:13-2:3.

For Further Study:
Try beginning an outline of 1 Peter on a separate sheet of paper. First, read the Study Skill on outlining on page 18. Then, either sketch out a broad outline of the whole book, or just outline 1:3-12.

11. You can help to assure that you understand a passage of Scripture by summarizing its main teaching. In lesson one, question 5, you gave a title to 1:3-12. After studying the passage more closely, how would you summarize it in a sentence?

_____

_____

_____

_____

_____

_____

12. List any questions you have about anything in this lesson.

_____

_____

_____

_____

_____

For the group

It's often easier to get a discussion moving if you begin with a simple question about group members' lives. Sharing about the past in early lessons helps to lay a foundation for sharing about the present later. For this lesson, you might begin by asking members to explain briefly one trial they had to endure in the past. (Of course, don't insist if someone prefers not to share.)

Next, ask someone to read 1:1-12 aloud. Then have several people summarize what they think Peter says in 1:1-12, to give focus to your discussion.

Peter mentions several topics in 1:1-12 that could become studies in themselves, such as new birth, hope, inheritance, joy, and the purpose of suffering. This lesson is designed to be an overview of the whole passage, rather than an in-depth study of any topic. Feel free to take a meeting for a topical study if you all agree, but otherwise avoid getting sidetracked. For instance, instead of discussing what you learned from each cross-reference in questions 4 and 5, you could bring them all into a discussion of question 6. Likewise, take five minutes to compare your inheritance (question 7) to competing goals in your lives (question 8). Then move to joy and the prophets and angels.

Try to follow Peter's train of thought. For instance, question 9a notes the connection between 1:3-5 and 1:6-9. Keep moving toward the overall point you think Peter is trying to make in 1:1-12.

The Optional Application questions give you a chance to apply parts of the passage as you go along. Or, you could interpret the whole passage first, and then discuss some of the Optional Applications or let members share responses to question 11.

Sharing applications offers a chance to get to know each other better, and suggests topics for group prayer. You might want to discuss possible ways of applying Scripture to yourselves, in case anyone is unfamiliar with application. Then pray for each other, asking God to enable you to take what Peter says to heart.

1. Erich von Eicken and Helgo Lindner, "Apostle," *The New International Dictionary of New Testament Theology,* Volume 1, edited by Colin Brown, (Grand Rapids, Michigan: Zondervan Corporation, 1975), page 128.
2. W.E. Vine, *An Expository Dictionary of New Testament Words* (Nashville, Tennessee: Royal Publishers, 1952), pages 989-990.
3. Kelly, page 44; Stibbs, pages 72-73.
4. Wuest, page 17.
5. Hartmut Beck and Colin Brown, "Peace," *The New International Dictionary of New Testament Theology,* Volume 2, pages 776-783; Markus Barth, *Ephesians 1-3,* Anchor Bible Volume 34 (Garden City, New York: Doubleday and Company, Incorporated, 1974), page 74.
6. Kelly, pages 46-47.
7. Vine, pages 988-989.
8. "Joy," *The Shorter Oxford English Dictionary,* Volume 1 (Oxford: Oxford University Press, 1973), page 1138.
9. Lawrence Crabb, *Effective Biblical Counseling* (Grand Rapids, Michigan: Zondervan Corporation, 1977), page 76.
10. Kelly, page 58; Vine, page 1067.

1 PETER 1:13-2:3

Consequences of Rebirth

Read 1:13-2:3, preferably in at least two translations. You might also skim this lesson, noticing definitions, subtitles, and so on. (Think about how the subtitles and your titles in lesson one, question 5 might help you outline 1:13-2:3.)

> **Study Skill—What's the Point?**
> In lesson two, you summarized 1:1-12 after studying it in detail. During your study, you used your titles from lesson one to help you read in context. However, it can also help to look for a passage's main message right before you study in detail.
> The key question here is, "What's the point?"[1] That is, 1) What is Peter talking about in this passage, and 2) Why is he saying it here (what does it have to do with what comes before and after)? In 1:13-2:3, for instance, Peter is not making random statements about God, Christ, and Christians. He has chosen what he says to make a point, to fulfill his goals for this letter.

1. What seems to be the point of 1:13-2:3? (Consider the whole passage, and what Peter talked about in 1:1-12. The connecting word "therefore" in 1:13 is a clue.)

   _____

   _____

_____

_____

_____

Holiness (1:13-16)

_____

Prepare your minds for action (verse 13). Literally, "gird up the loins of your mind." To gird the loins was to tuck one's long garment into one's belt so as to be free to move for flight or battle.[2]

Self-controlled (verse 13). "Sober" in NASB and RSV. "Of sound mind;"[3] that is, not drunk or deluded.

_____

2. Paraphrase the following phrases from 1:13. Explain what you think they mean.

a. "Prepare your minds for action."

_____

_____

_____

_____

_____

_____

b. "Set your hope fully on the grace to be given you when Jesus Christ is revealed."

_____

_____

_____

_____

_____

_____

Conform (verse 14). As in Romans 12:2, the Greek word *suschematizo* means "to shape one thing like another" and describes "what is transitory, changeable, unstable." This differs from *summorphizo* in Philippians 3:10, which describes a conforming of what is "essential in character and thus complete or durable, not merely a form or outline. *Suschematizo* could not be used of inward transformation."[4]

Holy (1 Peter 1:15). "Set apart" for God's purposes. The holy/divine/immortal was considered to be on a different plane from what is human/earthly/mortal. Holy people and things—priests, the Temple, the congregation, and so on—were devoted to worship of the Holy One. Ethical purity was central to the Jewish and Christian concept of holiness.[5]

For Further Study: Try a word study on *holy* and *holiness*. Begin with either New or Old Testament references in a concordance. You might also look at a Bible dictionary.

For Thought and Discussion: How is it possible to stop conforming to the world's habits, assumptions, and goals? How do we become holy? Think about 1 Peter 1:3-15; Ephesians 4:22-24; John 14:26, 15:1-2.

3. What is the difference between conforming to the desires of ignorance (verse 14) and being holy in all you do (verse 15). (*Optional:* See Romans 6:19, 8:5, 12:1-2.)

conforming _____

_____

_____

_____

_____

being holy _____

_____

_____

_____

_____

_____

For Further Study:
a. Examine other references to the fear of the Lord, such as Proverbs 9:10; Hebrews 12:28-29; 1 Peter 2:17, 3:15.
   b. On God's character as *Father*, see Luke 11:11-13, 15:11-32. On His character as *Judge*, see Matthew 7:1-2,21-23; 25:31-46; Luke 19:11-27.

Judgment (1:17)

Reverent fear (verse 17). The original Greek just says "fear," but NIV renders the intent of the word. In the Old Testament, "the fear of the Lord" is not terror of punishment for the slightest broken rule. Rather, it is awe in the face of the holy, the all-powerful, the utterly good and just. "Fear of man," says Proverbs 29:25, "will prove to be a snare," and fear of earthly things paralyzes the will and cripples courage (Luke 12:4-7,27-34). But "the fear of the LORD is a fountain of life," "a secure fortress," a source of contented rest (Proverbs 14:26-27, 19:23).

---

4. In verse 17, Peter connects two facets of God's nature—He is our Father as well as our impartial Judge. What does each of these facets mean to you?

Father _____

_____

_____

_____

Judge _____

_____

_____

_____

Redemption (1:18-21)

Redeemed (verse 18). "Ransomed" in RSV. The image is of someone freeing a slave by buying him from his master, or of a kinsman buying back property that a debtor has been forced to sell, or of someone paying a criminal's fine to release him from a death sentence (Exodus 21:8,30; Leviticus 25:25).

---

5. Describe the slavery from which Christ redeemed you personally (verse 18). (For instance, how was your own life "empty"— "futile" in RSV—before submitting to Jesus?)

_____

_____

_____

_____

_____

_____

_____

6. What important truths do verses 18-21 teach about . . .

Christ? _____

_____

_____

_____

_____

God? _____

_____

_____

_____

7. "For you know that" in verse 18 (NASB: "knowing that") implies that verses 18-21 should motivate us to live in godly fear. Why should knowing verses 18-21 move us to seek holy characters?

_____

_____

**Optional
Application:** Think of
a Christian brother or
sister for whom you
have difficulty feeling
love. Through prayer,
seek ways of living
sincere (unhypocriti-
cal, unpretended),
Christlike love toward
that person.

_____

_____

_____

Love because . . . (1:22-25)

In 1:15-21, Peter has been giving reasons for holiness: because God is holy (1:16), because judgment
is coming (1:17), and because Christ's blood has
redeemed us (1:18-21). Now, in 1:22-25 Peter turns
to give a reason for love.

___

Purified (1:22). From the same Greek root as "sanctifying" in 1:2.

Love for your brothers. *Philadelphia*, from *phileo*—
tender affection, feelings of closeness and
kinship.

Love one another. *Agapao*—Godlike and Christlike
love that chooses to sacrifice self for the
beloved's good, that takes no account of the
beloved's worthiness (John 15:12-13; 1 John
3:16-18, 4:9-11).[6]

Deeply (NASB: "fervently"). Indicates fervent action
rather than fervent feeling.[7]

Heart. To Jews and Greeks, the heart was the center
of will, emotions, and intellect.[8]

___

8. What do you think Peter's point is in 1:22?
Paraphrase the verse.

_____

_____

_____

_____

_____

_____

40

9. In your own words, explain what verses 23-25 teach.

_____

_____

_____

_____

_____

10. Why should this fact motivate us to fervent, Christlike love?

_____

_____

_____

_____

Babies (2:1-3)

This paragraph seems to continue the thoughts of new birth, holy life, and the Word from chapter 1.

Rid yourselves (verse 1). Literally, "putting off." In early Christian practice, removal of clothing before baptism signified rejection of a pagan lifestyle, and putting on white robes after baptism symbolized clothing oneself with Christ's character.[9] (Ephesians 4:22,24; Colossians 3:9,10,12; and James 1:21 have the same image.)

---

11. Are the vices of 1 Peter 2:1 primarily attitudes of the heart or outward actions? Why do you think so?

_____

_____

_____

Optional Application: Can you recall a recent time when you felt or showed one of the vices in 2:1? If so, what might have been the source of that "bad fruit" (Matthew 15:10-20, Luke 6:43-45, Galatians 5:13-26)? What can you do about this fruit?

12. Write the meaning of each vice listed in 2:1. (Consult a dictionary if necessary.)

malice _____

_____

_____

_____

deceit _____

_____

_____

_____

hypocrisy _____

_____

_____

_____

envy _____

_____

_____

_____

slander _____

_____

_____

_____

Study Skill—Changing Character
Sometimes the Bible commands a character trait, an attitude, or a habit which we find we cannot adopt by an act of effort or even much prayer. You may feel this is true about some of the traits listed in 1 Peter 2:1. One problem might be the "old self."

(continued on page 43)

(continued from page 42)
Before we knew Christ, we believed lies about how the world worked. We made choices based on those lies and built up a structure of habits and responses. Now that we know Christ, we have rejected those lies, but the structure remains. Paul talks about this predicament in Romans 7:22-24. He says that our only route to freedom from this structure is "through Jesus Christ our Lord" (Romans 7:25). We must let Him nail to the Cross the "old self" (Romans 6:6, Ephesians 4:22-24), the structure which fights to live on in our members. Letting Him do this involves asking Him to do it, giving Him permission to do it, having others pray for us (James 5:16), and acting in faith that God really has answered our prayer for freedom (Romans 8:2).[10]

Tasted that the Lord is good (verse 3). This quotation from Psalm 34:8 is used in some of the earliest Christian liturgies (written worship services) that scholars have found. In those services, it refers to tasting Christ in the Lord's Supper. However, its meaning in Psalm 34:8 is wider.[11]

---

13. "Spiritual" in verse 2 is *logikos* from *logos*, meaning "word." What "spiritual milk," or "milk of the word" (NASB), might Peter be urging his readers to crave? Think of as many possibilities as you can. (Hebrews 5:12-6:5 and John 6:53-56 may help you.)

_____

_____

_____

_____

_____

For Further Study:
Try outlining 1:13-2:3,
even if you did not
begin an outline of
1:1-12.

Your response

14. Reread your answer to question 1 of this lesson.
    If you have changed your mind about the main
    point of 1:13-2:3 after studying the passage in
    detail, write your new view here.

    _____

    _____

    _____

    _____

    _____

15. a. Did you find in 1:13-2:3 any specific truth
    about God, Christ, or yourself that you want
    to meditate on this week because it seems
    especially important to you? If so, write down
    what impresses you most from what Peter
    says in this passage. Pray that God would be-
    gin to make this truth take root in your heart
    and affect your character.

    _____

    _____

    _____

    _____

    _____

    _____

    _____

    b. Peter gives several commands in this passage.
    Choose one, and plan out some steps you
    could take to grow more obedient to this
    command in the coming week.

    _____

    _____

    _____

    _____

44

_____

_____

_____

16. List any questions you have about 1:13-2:3.

_____

_____

_____

_____

For the group

When we think of our Father and Judge, it is easy to imagine Him as our earthly fathers were. You might launch your discussion by asking members to describe briefly how they tend to think of God the Father. Then let members summarize the main point of the passage.

You could structure your discussion like this:

1. What is God like and what has He done, according to this passage?
2. Based on this, how should we relate to Him (children to Father)?
3. What are the specific implications (commands) of this relationship for how we think and act? Consider what each instruction in the passage (be self-controlled, be holy, etc.) means.
4. What do God's nature and commands seem to be asking of you currently?

Whole books have been written on the subject of how to grow in holiness, and much Scripture deals with it. Jerry Bridges' *The Pursuit of Holiness* and *The Practice of Godliness* (NavPress), and John and Paula Sandford's *The Transformation of the Inner Man* (Bridge) are good treatments of this subject.

How might you help each other to apply God's Word—to become holy or to prepare for action? How might you apply 1:22 in your group?

45

At the end of your meeting, you might pray to see your Father clearly, and ask to be able to love and obey Him as He is. Peter doesn't say much about relying on God's grace, but he assumes it.

Persecution in the Roman Empire

If 1 Peter is like most letters, it was written to address some particular situation in the lives of its sender and recipients. To understand the letter properly, we ought to come as close as we can to understanding what that situation was. We look first for clues in the letter itself.

Since Peter says a great deal about "grief in all kinds of trials" (1:6) and "the painful trial you are suffering" (4:12), we conclude that the Christians in Asia Minor were suffering. How were they suffering? Peter says that pagans were accusing them of doing wrong (2:12), speaking "maliciously against [Christians'] good behavior in Christ" (3:16), finding it "strange" that Christians did not participate in "dissipation" (4:4), insulting them "because of the name of Christ" (4:14), and making them "suffer as a Christian" (4:16). Peter stresses that his readers are "aliens and strangers" in the world (2:11, 1:1), and exhorts them repeatedly not to "conform" to pagan ways (1:14, 4:1-4). Peter does not mention legal trials, executions, or any conflict with the Roman government; indeed, he says that Roman governors are sent by the king "to punish those who do wrong and to commend those who do right" (2:14).

These clues coincide with the little else we know of relations between Christians and pagans in the 60s AD. Even after Nero's persecution of Christians in Rome, there seems to have been no law against being a Christian.[12] The fire gave some bigoted Romans a chance to persecute a defenseless minority, but there were evidently no similar organized witch hunts for Christians elsewhere in the Empire. However, people in smaller cities had the same reasons to be prejudiced against Christians that people in Rome had. (See "How Pagans Viewed Christians" on page 96.) Provincial cities tended to be small and

(continued on page 47)

46

(continued from page 46)

crowded with dozens of ethnic, economic, and religious groups. Members of a given group were close-knit; to betray one's family traditions was scandalous. Groups often jealously competed for economic or social status. Christians were not only outsiders in a neighborhood (and so probably discriminated against by landlords, employers, and salespeople), but also often traitors to their families' customs.[13]

Under Roman law, any private free person could accuse anyone else of a crime before the provincial governor. The governor had a fairly free authority to decide a case when there was no clear statute. We know that in 111-112 AD the governor of Bithynia and Pontus was plagued by people accusing their neighbors of being Christians. The governor, Pliny, often found that the Christians were not guilty of the "disgraceful practices"[14] that were rumored about them. Yet at first he went ahead and executed anyone who refused to deny Christ, because refusing to submit to the governor's order was *contumacia*— contempt of court.[15] Later however, Pliny wrote to his emperor for instructions because he could find no law against Christianity and because Christians seemed to be guilty of nothing worse than "a perverse superstition which went beyond all bounds."[16] Pliny's letter suggests that in 111 AD Christianity was legal but extremely offensive to pagans, and that many citizens thought Christians such a blot on society that they should be exterminated. Thus while there was no imperial law against the faith, there was strong feeling and action against it on the local level. It is little wonder that Peter urged "submission" to the authorities (short of betraying Christ) and exemplary behavior before pagans (2:12-13, 3:16). The government was the Christians' only defense against popular persecution.

---

1. Gordon D. Fee and Douglas Stuart, *How To Read the Bible for All Its Worth* (Grand Rapids, Michigan: Zondervan Corporation, 1982), page 24.
2. Kelly, pages 65-66.
3. Vine, page 1057.
4. Vine, page 219.

5. "Holy" in *The New International Dictionary of New Testament Theology*, Volume 2, pages 224-232.
6. "Love," *The New International Dictionary of New Testament Theology*, Volume 2, pages 538-550; Vine, pages 692-694.
7. Kelly, page 80.
8. Vine, pages 536-537; "Heart," *The New International Dictionary of New Testament Theology*, Volume 2, pages 180-184.
9. Kelly, pages 83-84.
10. John and Paula Sandford, *The Transformation of the Inner Man* (Plainfield, New Jersey: Bridge Publishing Company, 1982), pages 23-27.
11. Kelly, pages 86-87.
12. Bruce, page 422.
13. Ramsay MacMullen, *Paganism in the Roman Empire,* (New Haven: Yale University Press, 1981), pages 2-34.
14. "Pliny to Trajan" in Pliny, *Epistles*, x,96-97. See Bruce, page 423.
15. "Pliny to Trajan." See Bruce, pages 423,426.
16. "Pliny to Trajan." See Bruce, page 424.

1 PETER 2:4-10

God's Chosen

Read through 2:4-10, and prepare to study as you did in lesson three. Pray for understanding of what Peter is saying and how it should affect you.

> **Study Skill—Key Words**
> In 1:3-12, Peter talked about our "living hope." In 1:13-2:3, he described how we should act in light of that hope, and focused on God's "living word" (1:23). Now in 2:4-10, he talks about "living stones." Key words and phrases like these are clues to Peter's train of thought.

1. What seems to be the point of 2:4-10? (Consider how the passage relates to 1:13-2:3 and 2:11-12.)

_____

_____

_____

_____

_____

Living stones (2:4-8)

2. Observe everything Peter says about Jesus in

49

2:4-8, even seemingly trivial things. Write down what you observe.

_____

_____

_____

_____

_____

_____

_____

_____

_____

Cornerstone (verse 6 and verse 7 footnote). The most important stone in a building's foundation. A ***capstone*** (verse 7, NIV) is the central stone in an arch, which balances the arch's forces so that it will stand.

Study Skill—Metaphors
"Living Stone" (verse 4) is a figure of speech called a *metaphor.* A metaphor sheds new light on something by simply referring to it as something else—"All the world's a stage"—in order to imply a comparison between the two (usually dissimilar) things. The reference is not intended to be taken literally. Christ is not a literal stone, of course; Peter is simply trying to tell us something about Him by using this image.

3. What do you learn about Jesus from the metaphors "living Stone," "cornerstone," and "capstone"?

_____

_____

_____

_____

_____

_____

_____

_____

4. Explain in your own words what verse 6b means to you: "and the one who trusts in him will never be put to shame [NASB: disappointed]."

_____

_____

_____

_____

_____

_____

_____

Study Skill—Similes
A *simile* is a figure of speech that uses "like" or "as" for comparison. In verse 5, Peter says Christians are "like living stones" to show that we are like Jesus in certain ways.

Spiritual (verse 5). Not *logikos* as in verse 2, but *pneumatikos*, from *pneuma*, meaning "spirit" or "Spirit." Thus, the house and the sacrifices are of or for the (Holy) Spirit or our (human) spirits.

5. We Christians are "like living stones" being built into a "spiritual house" (verse 5). What does this image imply about how you should

view yourself, other Christians, and the Church as a whole? (*Optional:* See 1 Corinthians 3:9-16, Ephesians 2:19-22.)

_____

_____

_____

_____

_____

_____

_____

_____

A chosen people (2:5,9-10)

All of these images evoke Old Testament descriptions of Israel.

Priesthood (verses 5,9). When God first spoke to the Israelites just after delivering them from Egypt, He told them, "Now if you obey me fully and keep my covenant, then out of all nations you will be my treasured possession. Although the whole earth is mine, you will be for me a kingdom of priests and a holy nation" (Exodus 19:5-6). But within the kingdom of priests, God set apart a family of priests. He did this partly to show Israel what being priests for the nations meant, and partly to prepare against Israel's inevitable failure to keep covenant and the resulting need for a perfect Priest and Sacrifice, Jesus (Hebrews 9:6-10:14).

The duty of the priests in the Jerusalem Temple was to offer sacrifices of animals, grain, wine, oil, salt, incense, and prayer. The sacrifices were meant: 1) to honor God as God, 2) to cover the people's sins so that they could remain in relationship to Him, 3) to signify thanks for blessing, and 4) to petition God for

continuing graciousness. Priests offered sacrifices each morning and evening for the nation,
with extra offerings on feast days. In addition,
they were constantly making private offerings
on behalf of individuals who wanted to give
thanks, fulfill a vow, or atone for a sin (Leviticus 1-9,16,23-24).

The Law required priests to be free of
physical defects and ritual uncleanness (such as
contact with a corpse), to symbolize the purity
and perfection of holiness (Leviticus 21). Priests
were consecrated (set apart for holy service) by
washing with water and sprinkling with the
blood of a sacrificial animal (Exodus 29:21;
Leviticus 8:6,30; Hebrews 10:22). Priesthood
could not be earned; it came to all physically
whole adult males descended from Aaron.

6. What are "spiritual sacrifices" (Psalm 51:17;
   Romans 12:1, 15:15-16; Hebrews 13:15-16)?

   _____

   _____

   _____

   _____

   _____

   _____

Praises (verse 9). "Excellencies" (NASB) or "mighty
deeds."[1]

7. If you and all Christians are a "holy priesthood,"
   what does this identity imply about your . . .

   relationship toward God? _____

   _____

   _____

   _____

purpose in life? _____

_____

_____

_____

relationships with other Christians? _____

_____

_____

_____

relationships toward unbelievers? _____

_____

_____

_____

8. Explain 1 Peter 2:10. How have Christians
become "the people of God"? (*Optional*: See
John 1:12-13; Ephesians 2:4-6,11-16.)

_____

_____

_____

_____

_____

Royal priesthood (1 Peter 2:9). Jesus is both the
King of creation (Ephesians 1:9-10, Philippians
2:9-11) and the High Priest who offered Himself
as the perfect sacrifice for our sins (Hebrews
4:14-5:9, 7:11-10:18). By being reborn as God's
children and heirs (Romans 8:16-17, 1 Peter
1:3-4), we have entered Jesus' royal and priestly
family.

9. Reflect on what it means to be "a chosen people, a royal priesthood, a holy nation, a people

belonging to God" (1 Peter 2:9). What implications, other than those you have already mentioned, might this identity have for your life?

_____

_____

_____

_____

_____

_____

_____

For Further Study:
Do a word study on *chosen people* or *priest,* using a concordance. Find at least five Old Testament references, or more if you have time. What light do these Old Testament concepts throw on your identity in Christ?

> **Study Skill—Purpose**
> In questions 3 and 6 of lesson one, you examined Peter's purpose for writing the letter. Keeping this purpose in mind can help you identify the point of a passage. Ask yourself, "How does this passage fit into Peter's overall aim?" Of course, you may decide that a writer's main aim isn't what you thought it was, or that he had several aims.

10. Now that you have studied 2:4-10, try to summarize it in a sentence. (Think about its context—the purpose of the letter and Peter's train of thought so far.).

_____

_____

_____

_____

_____

11. Think about who Christ is and who you are, as described in 2:4-10. Which of Peter's statements most motivates you? Write it down, along with one important implication it has for your life. If this implication calls for you to take any practical steps, write them down also.

For Further Study:
Make up your own
outline for 2:4-10, or
all of 1:1-2:10.

_____

_____

_____

_____

_____

_____

_____

_____

Study Skill—Outlining

Below are two possible outlines for 1:1-2:10.
You might think about the merits of each
view.

1) Purpose of the book: To instruct groups of
believers, including some who are young in their
faith, "in the practical consequences of living out
the Christian faith, and to warn them how to cope
with trials and sufferings."[2]

1:1-2 Opening address
1:3-9 Salvation: its nature
1:10-12 Salvation: its revelation
1:13-5:4 Salvation: its practical outworkings
    1:13-21 Holiness of life
    1:22-25 Love for the brethren
    2:1-3 Desire for spiritual growth
    2:4-10 Membership of God's people
    (and so on, 2:11-5:4)

2) Purpose of the book: To encourage and
strengthen believers during a time of severe trial.
The theme is "Christ our hope and example amid
trial."[3]

Address (1:1-2)
The living hope—and what goes with it
    (1:3-2:10)
    The "living hope" (1:3-12) and our
        reaction to it (1:13-21)
    The "living word" (1:22-25) and our
        reaction to it (2:1-3)
    The "living stone" (2:4) and our relation
        to it (2:5-10)

12. List any questions you have about 2:4-10.

_____

_____

_____

_____

_____

For the group

Begin by giving members a chance to relate one
incident when they were *chosen* for something as
children. In a minute or two each, let members describe how that experience felt. If someone can't
recall ever having been chosen, he or she could describe the feeling of *not* being chosen.

After you have read aloud and summarized
2:4-10, explore each of Peter's images. What does it
mean in general that we are living stones, a holy
priesthood, and so on? What might Peter's descrip-
tion of our identity and mission mean for you this
week?

Peter's images are collective; we are not just
individual stones, priests, or people. How can your
group reflect this fact? How might you seek to be
built together? What spiritual sacrifices might you
offer together? How could you treat each other as
royal and holy?

Let your closing prayer reflect 1 Peter 2:9.

1. Kelly, page 99.
2. David H. Wheaton, "1 Peter," in *The New Bible Commentary:
   Revised,* edited by Donald Guthrie, et al. (Grand Rapids, Michigan: William B. Eerdmans Publishing Company, 1970), pages
   1237-1238.
3. J. Sidlow Baxter, *Explore the Book*, Volume 6 (Grand Rapids,
   Michigan: Zondervan Corporation, 1966), pages 299,303.

1 PETER 2:11-17

Lifestyle Witness

Isolating 2:11-17 is probably not a natural way to
break up the book—most readers feel that at least
2:13-3:7 is a unit. Many feel that 2:11-12 introduces
this section, and that 3:8-4:10 is part of the same
train of thought. So to keep 2:11-17 in perspective,
read 2:11-3:7.

Study Skill—Commands in Context
It is important to read specific commands in
the context of what Peter says before and
after them. Look for *motives*, and for *descriptions* of who we are as Christians. Connecting
words like *for* and *so* point to motives; titles
like *strangers* and *servants* describe our
identity.

---

1. Read through 2:11-25 again. Below, list each
   title Peter uses to describe Christians, each way
   he *commands* them to behave, and each *motive*
   he gives for this behavior.

   Titles

   aliens and strangers (2:11)

Titles *(continued)*
Commands
abstain from sinful desires (2:11)
Motives
so that pagans will glorify God for your goodness (2:12)

2. What seems to be the point of 2:11-3:7? (Remember the purpose of the letter.)

_____

_____

_____

_____

_____

For Further Study: Look back at the summaries you gave to the paragraphs 2:11-12, 2:13-17, 2:18-25, and 3:1-7 (pages 15-16).
a. What is the main command of 2:13-3:6?
b. What does this command have to do with 2:11-12?
c. To understand the Old Testament imagery of "aliens and strangers," look up those words in a concordance. You could begin with Hebrews 11:1-16.

Dear friends (verse 11). Literally, "beloved." In Peter's day, this was a very uncommon way for nonChristians to address intimate friends, but it was common for Christians (Romans 12:19, 1 Corinthians 10:14, James 1:16, 1 John 2:7). Pagans often found this address amusing, impressive, or shocking.[1]

Strangers (2:11-12)

3. What does it mean that Christians are "aliens and strangers" (verse 11) in the world? (*Optional*: See Philippians 3:20-21; 2 Corinthians 5:1,20.)

_____

_____

_____

_____

_____

4. Think of as many practical implications of this fact for the way you live as you can. (*Optional*: See Luke 12:32-34, 2 Corinthians 5:6-9, 1 Peter 2:11-12.)

_____

_____

_____

61

**Optional
Application:** Can you
think of any "sinful
desires, which war
against your soul"
(1 Peter 2:11)? How
does remembering
that you are a
stranger in this world
and God's representa-
tive (2 Corinthians
5:20, 1 Peter 2:12)
help you to deal with
these desires?

_____

_____

_____

_____

Accuse you of doing wrong (verse 12). Very strong
words in Greek. (NASB translates, "slander you
as evildoers.") Kelly thinks the phrase suggests
that Christians "were the object of blind suspi-
cion and detestation, . . . victimization, possibly even police charges arising out of public
disorders."[2]

---

5. Explain in your own words the motive in 2:12
for living good lives.

_____

_____

_____

_____

Submission (2:13-25)

The New Testament concept of submission can be
difficult for modern people to grasp. The boxes
"Persecution in the Roman Empire" (pages 46-47),
"Social Structure in the Empire" (pages 65-66), and
"Status and the Gospel" (page 71) may shed some
light on it.

Submit (2:13,18; 3:1; 5:5). "A Greek military term
meaning 'to arrange [troop divisions] in military
fashion under the command of a leader.'"[3] In
non-military use, it was "a voluntary attitude of
giving in, cooperating, assuming responsibility,
and carrying a burden."[4]

---

6. How do you think the phrase, "for the Lord's sake" (verse 13), should affect the way we submit to authorities?

_____

_____

_____

_____

_____

_____

7. Explain in your own words the motive verse 15 gives for submitting to authorities.

_____

_____

_____

_____

_____

8. How should being "free men" (verse 16) affect how we submit?

_____

_____

_____

_____

9. How do you think being "servants of God" (verse 16) should affect the way we submit to people?

_____

_____

_____

_____

_____

For Thought and Discussion: Think of some motives for submission that would not be "for the Lord's sake" (verse 13).

For Thought and Discussion: Think about the purpose of imperial governors, according to Peter (verse 14).
a. What officials in our day, if any, do you think have the same purpose?
b. Consider 1 Peter 2:13-17, 20-23; Acts 4:18-20; and John 18:19-23. How do you think a Christian should respond when he thinks an official is not living up to his purpose? Do you think it makes a difference whether it is you or other people who are suffering injustice?

For Further Study: Search Romans 13:1-14 for motives and ways of treating people in authority.

For Thought and Discussion: In 2:13-25, do you think Peter leaves room for Christians to evaluate and comment on the ideas and decisions of people in authority? Why or why not?

Optional Application: You are a citizen with rights to vote and influence decisions, but you are subject to all laws as long as they are in effect. Think of some current issue that is important to you. How might you submit, honor, and live as a free person and God's servant with regard to this issue?

10. In Acts 4:18-20 and 5:27-29,41-42, Peter showed how he balanced "fear" for God and "honor" for rulers (1 Peter 2:17). Explain what you think each attitude meant in practice for Peter.

fear for God _____

_____

_____

_____

_____

honor for rulers _____

_____

_____

_____

_____

11. Choose one of the titles, commands, or motives from 2:11-17 that you listed in question 1. Let your choice be one that you especially want to apply to your own life. Pray about the implications of this passage for you, asking God to enable you to obey this command, live by this motive, or live up to this title. Ask Him also if there is anything you should do to respond to this teaching. You can write any insights or plans here.

_____

_____

_____

_____

_____

_____

_____

_____

64

12. List any questions you have about 2:11-17.

_____

_____

_____

_____

_____

Optional Application: Select a verse to meditate on for the next week. Explore its implications, and look for ways to act on it.

For the group

You might begin this discussion by giving each member a chance to describe briefly what he or she thinks his or her reputation among unbelievers is. Members might find this easier if they think of some specific unbelievers.

One way of approaching this lesson is to focus on *what* submission to authority *means*, and *why* we should do it. *How* to do something is often clearer once we understand what and why.

The group leader or some other member may want to look up the cross-references in the optional questions before your discussion, to give you a wider view of the Bible's teaching on submission.

Lessons six and seven are short if you omit all the optional questions. You might prefer to do some of the optional questions in each lesson, or you might try to cover both lessons in one meeting. Use extra time to review what you've learned or just to catch your breath.

Social Structure in the Roman Empire

Patriarchy was the model for all of Roman society. Under Roman law, the father of a family had "unrestricted power over all other members of the family, a power of life and death. Ordinarily no member of the family could have property of his own; all acquisitions made by family members belonged to the father." A family council or a "censor's" reprimand limited the father's "cruelty or arbitrariness,"[5] but the father's own

(continued on page 66)

65

(continued from page 65)
moral code was the only real check on his rule.

Slaves, wives, unmarried daughters, and "unemancipated" sons were all under the father's absolute power. Slaves included "not only artisans, labourers, domestic helps and clerks, but . . . the majority of teachers, doctors and 'professional' people generally."[6] A freed slave had certain duties to his former master. Most free men, widows, and other legally independent persons were "clients" of a "patron," who acted in some ways as father to them in a world where a person without powerful patronage was often helpless.

A handful of wealthy aristocrats controlled local affairs in most cities; these men owned most of the industry and surrounding land, held the key offices, and were the only voters. They and Rome appointed all the judges, tax collectors, and city employees. Thus, to secure justice, it was crucial to have an aristocrat (or someone close to him) as a patron.

People generally accepted this system as just. Independence, democracy, and individualism were not valued as much as order, prosperity, loyalty, and duty. Patrons and fathers varied in moral virtue, but many took their responsibilities seriously.

The crucial differences between New Testament submission and the pagan social order were 1) the attitudes behind obeying commands and accepting consequences for disobedience, and 2) the limits ("fear God, honor the king") on obedience.

1. Kelly, page 103.
2. Kelly, page 105.
3. Wuest, page 60.
4. Barth, page 710.
5. Adolf Berger, "Roman Law," *The Encyclopedia Americana*, volume 23 (New York: Americana Corporation, 1960), page 645.
6. Kelly, page 115.

LESSON SIX

1 PETER 2:18-25

Submit as Christ

There are just a few numbered questions in this lesson, so that you can choose some of the optional questions that interest you. Because 2:18-25 closely connects with 2:11-17, you might reread those verses before reading 2:18-25. You could also refresh your memory with questions 1 and 2 on page 59-61.

___

Respect (verse 18). Literally, "fear," as in 1:17 and 2:17. See the definition on page 38.

___

1. In what situation is it not commendable to endure suffering (2:20)?

___

___

___

2. a. When is it commendable to endure suffering (verses 19-20)?

___

___

___

___

For Further Study: In light of 1:17 and 2:17, describe the attitude with which you believe Peter wanted slaves to submit to masters. (For instance, what might he have meant by "fear"? Whom should slaves fear?)

Optional Application: Think of a recent time you experienced hurt from another person. How do you think Jesus might have responded in that situation? What attitudes about Himself and others would have enabled Him to respond like this?

For Further Study: To examine more closely how Jesus responded to persecutors, see Luke 23:26-46; John 18:7-11,19-24,28-38; 19:1-11.

b. Why (verses 19,21)?

_____

_____

_____

_____

_____

Christ's example (2:21-25)

Jesus modeled both the *character* and the *actions* of a commendable sufferer. As you study His example, think about your own relationships to those over you, whether parents, teachers, pastors, judges, or supervisors. Notice that the issue is not, "Who has the right to have power over me?" Rather, it is, "How should I respond to those who do have power over me?"

3. How did Jesus respond (verses 22-23) to . . .

verbal abuse? _____

_____

_____

_____

physical abuse? _____

_____

_____

_____

4. Jesus endured because He focused on the goal of His suffering (Hebrews 12:2; compare 1 Peter 1:13). What was the goal of Jesus' suffering (1 Peter 2:24-25)?

_____

_____

_____

_____

_____

_____

5. The statements below describe what it might mean to "bear up under the pain of unjust suffering" (1 Peter 2:19). With Christ's pattern in mind, decide whether you think each statement is true or false. Be able to support your conclusions with Scripture; some sample references for you to think about are given. (Note: you may want to tackle just one or two of these issues.)

T F   You should never try to escape from unjust suffering. (Luke 4:28-30; Acts 9:23-25,28-30. Also, Matthew 2:13-15; Acts 12:6-11, 23:1-10.)

T F   You should never try to escape from unjust suffering if escape would require you to harm someone. (1 Samuel 24:4-7, Nehemiah 4:15-20, Luke 6:27-31.)

T F   You should never try to escape from unjust suffering if you risk harming yourself. (Acts 9:23-25,28-30; 12:6-11; 23:1-10.)

T F   God can always draw good results from your suffering. (Romans 8:28.)

T F   God intends any suffering you experience and does not want you to pray for or seek escape from it. (Psalm 109:21-31; 116:1-11; Matthew 26:39,41.)

T F   You may always seek to know what purpose God might have for your suffering. (Proverbs 16:4, John 15:15.)

T F   You should endure unjust suffering without retaliating in actions, words, or thoughts. (Romans 12:14-21, 1 Peter 2:21-23.)

T F   You should never let anyone know you think your suffering is unjust. (John 18:23; Acts 5:40-42, 23:1-5, 25:8-11; Philippians 1:12-18.)

69

For Thought and Discussion: Jesus' death is not just an example for us (1 Peter 2:21); it actually empowers us to acquire His character (2:24). How does it do this? (See Romans 6:6-11, 8:1-11.)

For Thought and Discussion: How can Christians help each other to bear up under suffering?

Optional Application: Memorize at least one verse from 2:11-25. Set aside time each day for the next week to think about what it means and how you might apply it to the situations you are facing.

T F   There is no such thing as unjust suffering; you are a sinner, so you deserve your suffering. (Matthew 2:16, Luke 13:1-5, John 15:18-19, 2 Timothy 3:12.)

6. Can you think of any practical ways you could begin applying any insight you found in 2:18-25? How might you seek to grow in the attitudes or adopt the behavior Peter commends?

_____

_____

_____

_____

_____

_____

_____

_____

7. List any questions you have about 2:18-25.

_____

_____

_____

_____

_____

For the group

As a warm-up, ask the group to describe how they reacted the last time they recall having been treated unjustly.

Some of the discussion questions, especially in question 5, may be controversial. You may decide to assign someone to find more Scripture references. Try to see that your opinions are grounded in Scripture. If you don't know what Scripture says on some topic, you might ask yourself what your opinions are based on.

The group leader should tell the group ahead of time which statements in question 5 you will discuss, so that everyone will have time to prepare. You probably won't want to discuss more than one or two of them.

Group discussions on controversial topics give you a chance to practice Peter's instructions, such as 1:22, 2:1-3, and 3:8-9.

Don't let a debate over something theoretical keep you from taking time to discuss any specific situations you might be facing in which you can apply Peter's words. Even if no one is currently facing a severe trial, do take time to pray for the attitudes Peter is urging.

Status and the Gospel

A typical city of the Roman Empire was full of groups with conflicting interests. But people could not express their political views through voting, petitioning, legal assembly, or peaceful protest. Consequently, every so often the iron-workers or the Cretans or the dyers would riot to protest a threat to their livelihood (Acts 19:23-41 shows an example of this). City governments would quickly squash rebellions, but in most cities some group or other was usually just approaching the boiling point.

Thus, anyone urging social revolution obtained an eager hearing, and any movement that seemed revolutionary frightened and alienated the wealthy. The aristocrats were extremely conservative; as firmly as many modern people believe that "new" means "improved," those people believed that "new" meant "corrupted." They thought that the world was declining, not progressing, and so they trusted only old customs, old families, old books, old gods.[1]

Revolutionaries and aristocrats held the same system of values—power, possessions, and public admiration. They shared the same methods—propaganda and coercion. Peter's means (submission to people) and his ends (convincing people to submit to Christ) contradicted both revolutionaries and conservatives.

1. MacMullen, page 3.

1 PETER 3:1-7

Marital Relations

"Live such good lives among the pagans," Peter says in 2:12, and he then proceeds to describe those lives. "Submit," he tells us, to political authorities (2:13-17), to masters (2:18-25), and to husbands (3:1-6). Then he adds a command to husbands, lest they imagine that the obligations in marriage are all on one side.

In 3:1-7, Peter continues to take the existing social structure for granted. Individual hearts, rather than social customs, are his priority. In both Jewish and pagan law, women were minors under their husbands' full authority.[1] But while Jewish law let wives own property and established limits on divorce, physical abuse, and adultery by husbands, Roman law did not. Greek and Roman philosophers taught that women were "inferior beings, intermediate between freemen and slaves."[2] Because "submission" suggested voluntary obedience, non-Christian ethical teachers almost never used the word to describe a wife's attitude.[3]

Normally, wives, slaves, and other dependents followed the religion of the head of their household. Still, as long as they did not dishonor the household rituals, a pagan man often permitted his dependents to pursue their own religion as well. However, a dependent who wanted to change her lifestyle or to honor one god alone encountered serious opposition. For Jews, it was a capital offense even to suggest conversion to Christianity (Deuteronomy 13:6-10).

It's tempting to let our own prejudices color

73

what we notice in 3:1-7. But Peter's words are still a challenge to all of us to change our ideas about marriage. Ask God to give you fresh eyes and a teachable heart as you read 3:1-7. Read 2:13-3:7 to put 3:1-7 in context.

Wives (3:1-6)

1. What light does the phrase "in the same way" or "likewise" (verses 1,7) shed on marital relations?

_____

_____

_____

_____

_____

_____

2. What reason does Peter give for wifely submission (verses 1-2)?

_____

_____

_____

_____

Reverence (verse 2). As in 1:17, 2:17, 2:18, and 3:6, this is literally "fear." NASB translates it as "respectful." Recall the definition on page 38.

---

3. a. What is "reverence" (verse 2)? What attitudes does it include? (Use a dictionary if necessary.)

_____

_____

74

_____

_____

b. Toward whom should a wife be reverent?

_____

_____

c. How might she show reverence?

_____

_____

_____

_____

_____

4. In verse 6, Peter exhorts wives to imitate Sarah by not giving way to "fear." What do you think he means? That is, what wrong fear might he be contrasting with the reverent fear of verse 2?

_____

_____

_____

_____

_____

_____

_____

For Thought and Discussion: How might a wife apply submission, reverence, and doing what is right without fear when her husband . . .
a. asks her to do something she believes is unbiblical (Acts 5:1-10)?
b. hits her?
c. forbids her to attend church or read the Bible?
(You might consult some of the references in question 5 on pages 69-70.)

Sometimes pagan husbands were more angry than impressed by wives who suddenly became "pure" (verse 2; "chaste" in NASB and RSV). Such wives would no longer share in eating, drinking, and sex at feasts with friends and business acquaintances.

Gentle (verse 4). "Meek" in KJV and in Matthew 5:5. Toward God, gentleness is "that temper of spirit in which we accept His dealings with us as good, and therefore without disputing or resisting."[4] In the Old Testament, the meek are those

75

For Further Study:
Use this study of the word *gentle* as a model for your own word studies— defining the word from a dictionary and refining your under- standing from many cross-references. You might want to read the verses listed here, as well as other ref- erences to gentle- ness, to see if you agree with the word study given here.

Optional Application: How can you acquire the attitude of gentleness more fully? Consider the following approaches:

a. Pray that God will reveal to you any roots of stubbornness and aggression in you. Confess these areas to God, and then seek and accept His forgiveness. Ask God to uproot your fears, and believe that He will do so.

b. Meditate on verses like 1 Peter 3:4 and Matthew 5:5, and pray for gentleness.

c. Give God per- mission to give you situations in which you can practice gen- tleness. Can you see any already facing you?

who rely on God rather than their own strength to defend them against injustice.[5] Thus, gentle- ness (meekness) toward evil people means knowing that God is permitting the injuries they inflict, that He is using them to purify His elect, and that He will deliver His elect in His time (Isaiah 41:17, Luke 18:1-8).[6]

Gentleness is "opposite to self- assertiveness and self-interest." It stems from trust in God's goodness and control over the situation. The gentle person is at peace because he is "not occupied with self at all."[7] Gentleness is a work of the Holy Spirit, not of the human will alone (Galatians 5:23), and it is also a response to the believer's calling from God (Ephesians 4:2). Jesus called Himself meek (Matthew 11:29) and pronounced blessing on the meek (Matthew 5:5). Paul urged all Chris- tians to be meek (2 Timothy 2:25, Titus 3:2). Peter implied that even masters should be meek toward slaves (1 Peter 2:18; NIV: "considerate"; NASB: "gentle"), and all should be meek with unbelievers (1 Peter 3:15).

---

5. Describe in your own words the kind of beauty Peter commended (verses 3-4).

_____

_____

_____

_____

_____

Husbands (3:7)

6. Give some examples of how a husband might be "considerate" (verse 7; NASB: "understanding") of his wife.

_____

_____

_____

76

_____

_____

_____

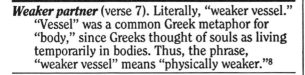

Weaker partner (verse 7). Literally, "weaker vessel."
"Vessel" was a common Greek metaphor for
"body," since Greeks thought of souls as living
temporarily in bodies. Thus, the phrase,
"weaker vessel" means "physically weaker."[8]

7. Why do you think each fact Peter mentioned
about women in verse 7 is important?

weaker vessel _____

_____

_____

co-heir of the grace of life _____

_____

_____

8. Why do you suppose failure to respect his wife
might hinder a man's prayers (verse 7)?

_____

_____

_____

9. a. What insight from 3:1-7 seems most significant to you currently?

_____

_____

For Further Study:
a. Study Paul's teach-
ing on marriage in
Ephesians 5:21-33.

b. Look at God's
original intent for
marriage (Genesis
2:18-25) and the
effect of the first sin
(Genesis
3:7,11-13,16).

**Optional
Application:** How
might Peter's com-
mand to husbands
affect your attitudes
and actions? Consider
how decisions are
made in your home,
how you communi-
cate, and so on.

For Further Study:
Try outlining 2:11-3:7.
You might want to
consider how
3:8-4:11 connects
with this passage.

_____

_____

_____

b. Is there any action you might take in light of
this insight? If so, write what you are plan-
ning to do—either to act in obedience, or to
build a character trait through meditation
and seeking God's grace.

_____

_____

_____

_____

_____

_____

10. List any questions you have about 3:1-7.

_____

_____

_____

_____

_____

For the group

Before you read 3:1-7 aloud, ask each woman in
your group to tell in one or two sentences what she
thinks a good husband is like. Also, let each man
tell what he thinks a good wife is like. Try not to
refer to Peter's words. Members' preconceptions will
offer an interesting comparison to Peter's teaching.
   Be careful to examine fully what Peter's words
mean before you begin applying them to modern
situations. Also, be sure to allow time for what Peter
says about husbands.

78

If you have time, discuss how a person becomes submissive and gentle. You might pray for the areas of each other's lives that are calling for submission, gentleness, or respect.

You are now about halfway through your study of 1 Peter. This might be a good time to consider how the study is going, and whether you want to do anything differently. At the end of your meeting you could simply ask, "What did you like best about this meeting?" and "What did you like least?"

1. Adolf Berger, "Roman Law," *The Encyclopedia Americana*, Volume 23 (New York: Americana Corporation, 1960), page 645.
2. Dwight M. Pratt, "Woman," *The International Standard Bible Encyclopaedia*, Volume 5, (Grand Rapids, Michigan: William B. Eerdmans Publishing Company, 1956), pages 3101,3103-3104.
3. Barth, page 710.
4. Vine, page 727.
5. Wolfgang Bauder, "Humility, Meekness," in *The New International Dictionary of New Testament Theology*, Volume 2, page 257.
6. Vine, page 728.
7. Vine, page 728.
8. Kelly, page 133.

1 PETER 3:8-22

Facing Mistreatment

As you read 3:8-22, think about how it relates to
what has gone before: the reminder of our hope; the
exhortation to holiness; the images of stones,
priests, and strangers; the commands to submit and
respect.

1. Recall the point of 2:11-3:7 (question 2, page
   61). What seems to be the point of 3:8-22?

   _____

   _____

   _____

   _____

   _____

Basic attitudes (3:8)

In verse 8, Peter lists five adjectives describing the
attitudes with which Christians should treat other
people, especially other Christians. These qualities
should underlie all our actions, but in this context
particularly our response to abuse. Peter urged
Christians to . . .

Live in harmony with one another. Literally, "be of
   one mind."

For Further Study:
a. Examine Jesus' examples of humility in Matthew 11:29; Luke 14:8-11; 22:24-27; John 13:3-5,12-17.
   b. Look through one of the Gospels for times when Jesus modeled one of the other traits listed in 1 Peter 3:8.

Be sympathetic. That is, "to enter into and share the feelings of others."[1]

Love as brothers. See page 40.

Be compassionate. Literally, "of good heart or affections."[2] In NASB, "kindhearted"; in RSV, "have . . . a tender heart."

Be . . . humble. Lowly. In the man-centered Greek world, lowliness/humility was considered "shameful"[3]—the cringing of a slave or a lack of self-respect. In the God-centered world of the Bible, however, lowering oneself is the first step to a right relationship with God and others. Jesus modeled the servant attitude He expected of His followers.

2. Why is harmony among Christians crucial? (*Optional*: See Matthew 18:19-20, John 17:21.)

_____

_____

_____

_____

_____

3. How can Christians disagree while maintaining harmony? Read at least one set of the following verses, and record Jesus' and Paul's teaching.

Attitude toward one's own rights (1 Corinthians 6:7, 9:10-12)

82

Attitude toward one's own righteousness
(Matthew 6:14-15, 7:1-3)

**Optional
Application:** How
might you show sym-
pathy and compas-
sion for some person
you know who is
grieving, poor, doubt-
ing the faith, or strug-
gling with sin?

How to settle disagreements (Matthew
5:21-24, 18:15-17, 1 Corinthians 6:1-6)

4. Which of the attitudes in 1 Peter 3:8 do you
find hardest to live by? Why do you think it is
so difficult for you?

_____

_____

_____

_____

_____

_____

**Optional
Application:** What
might you do this
week to "pursue"
peace (verse 11)?

For Further Study:
Paraphrase verse 13.
Do you think Peter
means that no one
will try to harm you if
you intend to do
good? See 2 Timothy
3:12.

Blessing for evil (3:9-17)

5. a. Peter tells us to give a "blessing" to those
who insult or injure us (3:9). What do you
think he means by this command? (*Optional:*
See Luke 6:27-38.)

_____

_____

_____

_____

b. Luke 6:35-36 and 1 Peter 3:9 give two reasons why we should bless those who insult
us. What are those reasons?

_____

_____

_____

_____

6. In 1 Peter 3:10-12, Peter is quoting Psalm
34:12-16. Explain in your own words what these
verses say we should do to attain joy in life and
answers to prayer. (Recall from page 25 the Jewish sense of "peace.")

_____

_____

_____

_____

_____

_____

7. What question should you always be prepared to
answer (verse 15)?

_____

_____

_____

8. Verse 15 tells us to "set apart" (NASB: "sanctify"; RSV: "reverence") Christ as Lord in our hearts. What does this have to do with returning blessing for insult, not fearing intimidation, and explaining the hope within us?

_____

_____

_____

_____

_____

_____

_____

Optional Application: How could you more faithfully set apart Christ as Lord of your thoughts and actions?

For Thought and Discussion: What does it mean to set apart Christ as Lord in your heart?

Motivation: Christ's victory (3:18-22)

"For" in verse 18 introduces the reasons for the teaching of verses 14-17. It explains why and how "you are blessed" if you "suffer for what is right" (verse 14).

9. First, why did Christ die (verse 18)?

_____

_____

_____

_____

Preached to the spirits in prison (verse 19). A difficult verse. Some interpreters believe Jesus went to the underworld between His death and resurrection, and preached the gospel to unbelievers of Noah's day. Others think Jesus proclaimed judgment to those dead unbelievers. (Against these interpretations, Irving Jensen asks, "why did not Christ preach to *all* unbelieving dead, of all time? Or if He did, why does Peter just cite those of Noah's day?"4)
    Another view is that "the preincarnate

85

For Further Study:
What do you think a
"good conscience"
(verses 16,21) is?
(You might consult a
Bible dictionary or a
commentary, or you
might use a concord-
ance to find other
scriptures about
conscience.)

Christ preached *through Noah* to unbelievers of his day."[5]

A third view is that "the preincarnate Christ preached to fallen angels."[6]

---

10. According to verses 20-21, Noah's experiences foreshadowed Christian baptism. How is baptism like Noah's adventure? (If necessary, read about Noah in Genesis 6:9-9:17).

_____

_____

_____

_____

_____

_____

11. Verse 21 says that baptism saves you not by removing physical dirt but by embodying your "pledge of a good conscience toward God" (NIV), or "appeal to God for a good conscience" (NASB, RSV). In this pledge or appeal, baptism involves you in Jesus' resurrection.

Read Romans 6:3-7. How does baptism . . .

identify you with Jesus' resurrection? _____

_____

_____

_____

_____

_____

appeal to God for a good conscience? _____

_____

_____

_____

_____

12. In 3:8-22, Peter seems to move from thought to thought by free association rather than step-by-step logic. Still, he follows a general structure: *Do this* (verses 8-9,14-17) for *these reasons* (verses 10-13,18-22).

Now that you've looked at this passage more closely, summarize in one or two sentences what now seem to be its main points. Keep the overall message of 1 Peter in mind.

For Further Study: "Angels, authorities, and powers" (verse 22) are names for various categories of spiritual beings. Look at Ephesians 1:2-21, 2:1-5, and Colossians 2:13-15. How did Christ conquer the spirits who used to control people?

For Further Study: Outline 3:8-22, fitting it into an outline of the whole book if you are working on one.

_____

_____

_____

_____

_____

_____

13. Consider the commands and reasons Peter gives in 3:8-22. Do any of them encourage you to concentrate on a particular area of your life for growth? If so, pray for grace to become more Christlike in this area and for guidance with any practical steps you might take in obedience to grace. After praying, write down anything further you believe you can do in this area.

_____

_____

_____

_____

_____

_____

14. List any questions you have about 3:8-22.

_____

_____

_____

_____

For the group

To get everyone thinking together, you might launch your discussion by asking members to describe the last time they were insulted for their beliefs.

Keep track of Peter's train of thought by summarizing 3:8-22, and then each of the three paragraphs: 3:8-12, 3:13-17, and 3:18-22. For instance, what point is Peter making by what he says about Christ in 3:18-22? The details of verse 19 are less important than what the paragraph has to do with the whole passage. After you have traced Peter's train of thought, you can go back to examine what key phrases ("harmony," "set apart Christ as Lord," etc.) mean. Keep trying to apply these statements to yourselves.

You might discuss what can get in the way of our doing what Peter says. For instance, what in us can make it hard to be humble or repay evil with blessing? How can we overcome those contrary goals, impulses, or whatever they are?

The group can be a good place to practice application. For example, how can you practice among yourselves the rules for community living of verse 8? How can you work with each other to pursue peace, set apart Christ as Lord, and so on?

You might also share a bit about how your efforts to apply past lessons are going. Consider discussing in pairs how your understanding of submission has affected your life so far. You may be able to help each other with any frustration or confusion that has surfaced.

1. Kelly, page 136.
2. Vine, page 857.
3. Hans-Helmut Esser, "Humility," *The New International Dictionary of New Testament Theology*, volume 2, page 260.
4. Jensen, page 68.
5. Jensen, page 68.
6. Jensen, page 68. See also Kelly, page 154; Stibbs, pages 142-143; Wuest, pages 97-99.

1 PETER 4:1-11

Suffering in the Body

Chapter 4 begins with "Therefore," which links 4:1-11 with 3:17-22. So, reread 3:17-22, and then read 4:1-11 slowly a couple of times. Compare your titles of 4:1-6 and 4:7-11 (page 16) to the subtitles in this lesson, and ask yourself what the best titles for these paragraphs would be.

Suffered (verse 1). In Christian creeds, Christ's "suffering" means His sacrificial death. (See Luke 24:46.)[1] Thus, 1 Peter 4:1 recalls Christ's victory over sin and over the spirits Peter mentioned in 3:22 and possibly 3:19. "Put to death in the body" (3:18) is equivalent to "suffered in his body" (4:1).[2]

Because he who has suffered in his body is done with sin (verse 1). Most commentators[3] think that 1 Peter 4:1 does not refer to the way God may use physical and emotional suffering to purge us from sin. God does sometimes use pain and hard times to teach reliance upon Him (Deuteronomy 8:1-3; 2 Corinthians 1:8-9, 12:7-10), but this is not Peter's topic.

Instead, "because . . . sin" probably refers to the identification with Christ mentioned in 1 Peter 3:21. In conversion, the Christian has united with Christ in His death ("suffering"), and so he shares in Christ's victory over evil (see Romans 6:3-7, Galatians 2:20).[4]

Living from Christ's viewpoint (4:1-6)

1. In 1 Peter 4:1, Peter exhorts his readers to "arm" themselves with an "attitude" (NASB: "purpose"; RSV: "thought") like Christ's.

   a. In what sense have you suffered and so finished with sin (verse 1)?

   _____

   _____

   _____

   _____

   b. What effect should that suffering have on how you approach the rest of your earthly life (verses 1-2)?

   _____

   _____

   _____

   _____

   _____

   _____

2. Not every nonChristian indulges the desires for illicit sex, alcohol, violence, and idolatry that Peter lists in verse 3. Even so, explain how an apparently "good" nonChristian (and at times a Christian as well) is nonetheless living for "evil human desires" (verse 2; NASB: "the lusts of men").

   _____

   _____

   _____

   _____

   _____

   _____

Those who are now dead (1 Peter 4:6). Two interpretations for this phrase have been suggested. Some people think that these dead are probably Christians who had died. The earliest Christians expected Christ to return very soon, and so they were dismayed when believers began to die and the Lord had still not come. Unbelievers taunted that these deaths proved that Christians did not have eternal life. (Paul responded to this concern in 1 Thessalonians 4:13-18.)

On this interpretation, Peter is encouraging his readers that their brothers "who are now dead" did not believe in vain. They were indeed "judged according to men in regard to the body" in that a) they suffered the physical death which all Adam's heirs must undergo, and b) they also suffered the ridicule of pagans who judged that they believed Christ in vain. Nevertheless, says Peter, when Christ returns to judge the living and the dead, the sleeping believers will be vindicated. They will "live according to God in regard to the spirit."[5]

Other people interpret 4:6 as referring to Christ's descent into hell to preach to those who had died before He came the first time.

3. In verses 5-6, how does Peter encourage believers who have to endure mocking from unbelievers? Explain in your own words.

_____

_____

_____

_____

_____

_____

The end is near (4:7-11)

4. Think about Peter's warning: "The end of all things is near" (verse 7). Then, in your own

91

words describe the state of mind and behavior
that confronting this fact should produce in us.

verse 7 _____

_____

_____

_____

verse 8 _____

_____

_____

verse 9 _____

_____

_____

verses 10-11 _____

_____

_____

_____

5. a. Why do you think the traits of verse 7 are
appropriate if the end of familiar life is
imminent?

_____

_____

_____

_____

b. Why should love (verse 8) be top priority for
Christians awaiting the end?

_____

_____

_____

_____

6. In Peter's day there were no "decent hotels for ordinary people,"[6] so hospitality to traveling Christians was crucial. There were no church buildings, so Christians had to open their homes for meetings. How do you think hospitality differs from entertaining?

_____

_____

_____

_____

_____

_____

For Thought and Discussion: Think about why guests might tempt a host to grumble (verse 9). What do the demands of hospitality reveal to you about love?

For Further Study: Study biblical hospitality on your own, beginning with passages like Genesis 18:1-8, 19:1-13; Deuteronomy 23:24-25, 24:19-22; Matthew 25:31-40; Hebrews 13:2.

Faithfully administering (verse 10). Literally, "as faithful stewards of." A steward was the slave in a household who kept affairs running and distributed food, money, and other needs to household members.

7. What does verse 10 tell you about why God gives gifts to us?

_____

_____

_____

_____

_____

8. What do you learn from verse 11 about the way a Christian should serve?

_____

_____

_____

_____

**Optional
Application:** Evalu-
ate your own attitudes
in serving, speaking,
offering hospitality, or
exercising some other
gift. Do verses 10-11
suggest any areas in
which you might
improve?

Gift (verse 10). As "gifts," Paul in various letters
lists prophecy, service, teaching, encourage-
ment, giving money and goods for others'
needs, leadership, showing mercy (Romans
12:6-8), wisdom, knowledge, faith, healing,
miracles, discernment of spirits, speaking in
tongues, interpretation of tongues (1 Corinthians 12:8-10), and so on. These lists are probably
not meant to be exhaustive; a gift might be
common or extraordinary, for public or quiet
use.

9. Think about the way of life Peter urges in
   4:1-11, and also the motives he gives, such as
   verses 1, 7, and 11. Is there anything in Peter's
   words that you think should make a difference
   in the way you act in your current circumstances? If so, write down how you would like
   this teaching to affect you, along with any steps
   you could take this week to better conform to
   Peter's picture of the Christian life. Try to focus
   on one area for growth, and look for ways to
   take on Christ's attitude in that area.

   _____

   _____

   _____

   _____

   _____

   _____

   _____

10. How would you summarize Peter's point in
    4:1-11?

    _____

    _____

    _____

    _____

11. Many people feel that Peter begins a second section of his letter in 2:11 with the words "Dear friends" (NASB: "Beloved"). He seems to end this section with the "Amen" in 4:11, and to begin again, "Dear friends" in 4:12.

Review your titles in lesson one, question 5 (pages 15-16), and skim over 2:11-4:11. Then try to summarize what you think this section is about. (You might ask yourself how 2:11-4:11 fits into the purpose of the letter, or what the most important words of the section are.)

_____

_____

_____

_____

_____

_____

12. List any questions you have about 4:1-11.

_____

_____

_____

_____

For the group

Before you read 4:1-11, ask everyone to describe briefly his or her lifestyle before committing to Christ—not a detailed story but a thumbnail sketch.

After summarizing the passage, give everyone a chance to respond if they wish to the interpretations of 4:1 and 4:6 in this study guide. Encourage anyone who feels strongly to research the issue or ask his pastor, but don't devote a lot of time to these issues. Gordon Fee comments that the epistles were not written to answer all of our questions, but only those the Holy Spirit decided we needed to understand. Humility includes accepting imperfect knowledge of matters like 1 Peter 4:6.[7]

As always, focus on the overall point Peter is making as you move through the questions.

There is a great deal to apply in this passage. You could either choose a few points to explore together, or let each person share what he or she hopes to take to heart.

How pagans viewed Christians

We have described the tension between pagan men and their newly "pure" wives (lesson seven, page 75). Christian men, too, faced "abuse" (4:4) when they abstained from normal social events. Civic patriotism and neighborliness in the Empire centered on elaborate festivals in honor of patron gods. The whole town would turn out to parade with banners and sometimes images of the gods, and in some cases there was cult prostitution or ritual self-mutilation. Christians and Jews, who naturally avoided these festivals, appeared anti-social, unpatriotic, and impious to their neighbors, to whom strict monotheism was unthinkable.

Most of a city's meat was sold at butcher shops attached to temples, which sold meat after sacrifices. Dinner parties were often held in private rooms attached to temples, and the god was honored as the feast's patron. The practices of 1 Peter 4:3 did not *always* occur at feasts, but they did at many. Hence, Christians offended their neighbors and business associates by declining invitations to dinner. Friends and business contacts soon shunned men who refused to eat with them.

Finally, pagans heard that Christians called each other "beloved," kissed each other (1 Peter 5:14), held "love feasts" and ate someone's body and blood (John 6:53, 1 Corinthians 11:17-29). These rumors gave rise to suspicions that Christians committed incest, cannibalism, and a catalogue of other vices at their secret meetings.[8]

1. See the marginal note to 1 Peter 4:1 in NASB, Acts 17:3, and Hebrews 13:12. See also Kelly, pages 119, 165.
2. Kelly, page 165; Stibbs, page 146.
3. Kelly, page 168; Stibbs, page 148; Wheaton, page 1245; Wuest, page 114.

4. A good passage to compare is Hebrews 5:7-9. Jesus became perfect and learned obedience "from what he suffered" (verse 8) partly in life but in fullness in accepting death on the Cross. *His* suffering unto death perfects us. By contrast, Hebrews 12:3-7 urges us to let God purify us through our own suffering, but we must do so with an attitude of identifying with Jesus. See also Romans 6:11-12, 8:12-14, and Colossians 1:24.
5. Kelly, pages 172-176; Stibbs, page 151.
6. Kelly, page 178.
7. Fee and Stuart, pages 55-56.
8. Bruce, page 425; Henry Chadwick, *The Early Church* (New York: Penguin Books, 1967), pages 23-29; MacMullen, pages 18-42.

1 PETER 4:12-19

Suffering for the Name

Many students feel that Peter is beginning a new section in 4:12 after the "Amen" in 4:11. Even so, he is still talking about our attitude under persecution in light of imminent judgment.

Read 4:12-19 slowly twice. Try to keep in mind what Peter has already said about suffering.

1. What is Peter's point in 4:12-19?

_____

_____

_____

_____

_____

2. In verse 12, Peter urges us not to be "surprised" when unbelievers misjudge and mistreat us.

   a. Why might a Christian find persecution surprising?

_____

_____

_____

_____

_____

b. Why should a Christian not be surprised at rejection and hurt because of his faith? (*Optional*: See John 15:18-25, James 1:2-4, 1 Peter 1:6-7.)

_____

_____

_____

_____

_____

Painful trial (1 Peter 4:12). Literally, "firing" (NASB: "fiery ordeal"). The Old Testament uses this word for the "refining of metals by fire . . . or, metaphorically, the testing of people."[1]

3. According to verse 13, why should Christians rejoice as they suffer? Explain in your own words.

_____

_____

_____

_____

_____

4. In 3:14-22, Peter explains why those who "suffer for what is right" are blessed. In 4:14 he explains why those who "are insulted because of the name of Christ" are blessed.

What do you think it means to suffer "because of the name of Christ"?

_____

_____

_____

Glory (verse 14). In the Old Testament, God's glory was the cloud of His Presence that rested upon the tabernacle or the Temple (Exodus 33:9-10, 40:34-35; Ezekiel 9:3, 10:3-4). The word signified "weight" and "brightness." Moses had to wear a veil over his face in public; his face shone when he had been near the Lord's glory in the tabernacle (Exodus 34:34-35).

The presence of God's glory is a promise and sign of the new covenant (Isaiah 60:1-3, Luke 9:28-36).

5. The blessing for suffering because of the name is that "the Spirit of glory and of God rests on you" (verse 14). What do you think this phrase means? (*Optional*: See Matthew 10:17-20, Acts 7:51-60, 2 Corinthians 3:5-18.)

_____

_____

_____

_____

_____

_____

6. Christians are supposed to proclaim Jesus as Lord (Matthew 28:19-20), expose the deeds of evildoers (Ephesians 5:11), and urge fellow Christians to repent when they stray (James 5:19-20). But Peter warns his readers that there is no glory in suffering as a criminal or as a "meddler" (1 Peter 4:15).

Can you offer any principles for how we can proclaim Jesus in word and deed without becoming meddlers? (*Optional*: See Galatians 6:1-5; 1 Peter 2:12-13,17-18; 3:1,15.)

_____

_____

For Thought and Discussion: Why do you think God will judge His people first (1 Peter 4:17)? See Ezekiel 9:3-6, Malachi 3:1-6, 1 Corinthians 11:32.

_____

_____

_____

_____

_____

_____

Family (verse 17). Literally, "house." Thus, either "household" (NASB, RSV) or God's "house"—the Temple (Ezekiel 9:3-6). The Church is both God's family and His holy dwelling (1 Corinthians 3:16, 1 Peter 2:5).

7. What do you learn about the Last Judgment from 1 Peter 4:17-18? Write down as many observations as you can.

_____

_____

_____

_____

_____

_____

_____

8. Peter sums up the implications of our coming judgment in verse 19.

a. First, we should entrust ourselves to our "faithful Creator." What might it mean in practice for you to entrust yourself to Him? (You might try to define for yourself what it means to entrust yourself, and then think about practical ways of doing this.)

_____

_____

_____

_____

_____

_____

_____

b. Second, we should "continue to do good"
   (NASB: "what is right," as in 2:20 and 3:17).
   How would you explain in your own words
   what it means to do right? (You might think
   about how we can find out what is right—
   Ephesians 2:10, 5:9-10; 2 Timothy 3:16.)

_____

_____

_____

_____

_____

9. Reflect for a few minutes on what Peter has said
   about the Judgment and its implications for us.
   Can you think of any practical ways in which
   you might act on one of those implications in
   the coming week? If so, write down any steps
   you might plan to take.

_____

_____

_____

_____

_____

_____

103

10. Is there some other insight from 4:12-19 that you hope to take to heart this week? If so, write it down, along with any plans you have for meditating on it or obeying it.

_____

_____

_____

_____

_____

_____

_____

11. List any questions you have about 4:12-19.

_____

_____

_____

_____

For the group

Since you've been studying about suffering for several weeks now, you might briefly share how your outlooks on your circumstances have changed. Have you had any chances to apply what you've been reading? How is it going? Would anyone in the group like prayer at the end of the meeting about some situation? You could share about this either before or after you discuss 4:12-19.

This passage offers a lot to pray about. You might pray for endurance under trials, and for God to prepare you and others for His Judgment. You might praise your "faithful Creator" and recommit yourselves to Him.

1. Kelly, pages 184-185.

1 PETER 5:1-7

An Orderly Community

This passage begins with the connecting word *Therefore* (NASB) to show that Peter's instructions to elders follow directly from his teaching in 4:12-19, and especially from 4:19. So reread 4:17-19, and then read 5:1-11 prayerfully. Also, read the box, "Early Church Leadership," on page 115.

Elders (5:1-4)

Witness (1 Peter 5:1). "One who testifies" (originally, in a court of law) to what he knows. Peter seems to imply that his readers were fellow-witnesses just as they were fellow-elders.

1. What does 5:1-7 have to do with Peter's point in 4:12-19, or with the overall aim of the letter?

   _____

   _____

   _____

   _____

   _____

   _____

   _____

2. The leader of the apostles could certainly have chosen a grander way to identify himself than he did in verse 1. Why do you suppose Peter calls himself "fellow. . ."? What motives and character traits does this choice suggest?

_____

_____

_____

_____

_____

Shepherds (verse 2). The image of the community's leaders as its shepherds came to Judaism and Christianity through the Old Testament prophets (Jeremiah 3:15, 10:21; Ezekiel 34:2-16). The tasks of a Near Eastern shepherd were:

    a. to *watch* for enemies trying to attack the sheep,

    b. to *defend* the sheep from attackers,

    c. to *guide* the sheep to food, water, and shelter,

    d. to *heal* wounded and sick sheep,

    e. to *find* and *save* lost or trapped sheep, and

    f. to *love* them, sharing their lives and so earning their trust.[1]

3. Draw analogies from the above list to what a person in spiritual authority should do for those he leads.

    a. _____

       _____

       _____

    b. _____

       _____

       _____

106

c. _____
_____
_____

d. _____
_____
_____

e. _____
_____
_____

f. _____
_____
_____

4. Name two wrong reasons for accepting leadership in a church (verse 2).

a. _____
_____

b. _____
_____

Considering what being known as a Christian did to a man's business and social life in Peter's day, we can understand why he might have only reluctantly agreed to be known as a Christian leader.

5. a. Might a modern Christian leader feel he is serving for the reason you named in question 4a? If you believe so, what might make him feel this way?

_____
_____
_____
_____

b. How might a modern church leader be tempted to the reason you wrote in question 4b?

_____

_____

_____

_____

_____

_____

6. a. What example does Peter want elders to set (verse 3)?

_____

_____

_____

_____

b. Look at question 2. How did Peter set this example?

_____

_____

_____

_____

7. How do you think members of the Church can make it easier for leaders to do their jobs? Give some practical suggestions for two of the following areas.

Shepherd the flock _____

_____

_____

_____

_____

_____

_____

Serve willingly _____

_____

_____

_____

_____

_____

Resist monetary temptations _____

_____

_____

_____

_____

_____

Not lord over members _____

_____

_____

_____

_____

Set an example _____

_____

_____

_____

_____

For Further Study:
Study Jesus' examples of humility in the references on page 82. Or, study other references, such as 1 Corinthians 8:1-3 or James 4:13-17. What other examples of humility can you find in Scripture? (You could just read through one of the Gospels or one of Paul's letters.)

Humility (5:5-7)

We should understand Peter's commands to wives, husbands, elders, and youth in the context of his words for all believers in 2:13, 4:8, and 5:5. Peter's society was ordered strictly by age, birth status, and gender. People were acutely conscious of how they had a right to be treated by each person they dealt with. Superiors were expected to lord it over inferiors. By contrast, Peter taught the ethic of humility, following Jesus' example. (See references to *humble* in 3:8, page 82.)

Clothe (verse 5). This "rare"[2] word comes from the overalls which slaves wore to keep clean while working, an exceedingly humble garment.

---

8. Toward whom should Christians humble themselves?

    5:5 _____

    5:6 _____

9. Study at least two of the following cross-references, and write down what you learn about humility.

    Luke 6:41-42 _____

    _____

    _____

    _____

    _____

    Luke 17:7-10 _____

    _____

    _____

    _____

    _____

Luke 18:10-14 _____

_____

_____

_____

_____

John 13:3-16 (Washing the grime off guests'
feet was the most despised task in the Jewish
household.)

_____

_____

_____

_____

Romans 12:3,16 _____

_____

_____

_____

_____

James 4:1-6 _____

_____

_____

_____

_____

10. From questions 8 and 9, how would you define
humility?

_____

_____

_____

_____

**Optional
Application:** How
might you go about
applying 1 Peter
5:6-7 to your relation-
ship with God this
week?

_____

_____

11. Think about what you know of God's character
    and His purposes for humanity. Why do you
    suppose He "opposes the proud but gives grace
    to the humble" (1 Peter 5:5)? (*Optional:* See
    Exodus 20:2-6; Matthew 11:29; 20:25-28;
    Romans 1:18,21.)

_____

_____

_____

_____

_____

_____

Cast (verse 7). Literally, "casting." Verse 7 depends
upon verse 6.

12. Why is casting all your anxiety on God (1 Peter
    5:7) an action of humility?

_____

_____

_____

_____

13. Think of one or two practical ways in which you
    could "clothe" yourself with humility toward
    another person this week—someone toward
    whom you have difficulty *feeling* humble.

_____

_____

_____

_____

_____

_____

14. According to verse 7, why is it safe for us to entrust our fears and our status to God? Explain in your own words.

_____

_____

_____

_____

_____

15. Is there any other response you might make to anything in this lesson? Are you moved to meditate on a verse, pray consistently about something, confess and seek grace to change a habit, or take some more active step in your dealings with another person? If any plans come to mind, write them down here, to help you remember.

_____

_____

_____

_____

_____

_____

16. List any questions you have about 5:1-7.

_____

_____

_____

_____

For Thought and Discussion: a. From Jesus' example and from 1 Peter 5:1-4, describe some ways in which a humble leader differs from one who is either proud or insecure.

b. Review what you learned from 2:13-3:22 about submission. How does a humble servant serve differently from one who feels fearful or worthless?

For the group

This lesson deals with the double strand of church order: humble leadership and humble submission to leadership. It is a long lesson because humility is so central to Jesus' teaching. As always, you should feel free to leave some questions for further study if time is limited. The most important thing is to grasp Peter's overall message; you can delve deeper later on your own.

Most people have known a situation in which church harmony broke down and hurt people either because leaders weren't humble and gentle, or because followers weren't humble and responsibly submissive, or both. You might open your discussion by letting the group briefly explain any fears or bad experiences they have had as leaders or followers. This may lay a basis for discussing how leaders and followers *should* act.

After you interpret Peter's words, you might talk about how Christians should deal with those situations when leaders and followers clash. Should followers do what they are told no matter what? Why or why not? How should a church deal with leaders who are abusing their power? How should a church deal with followers who won't submit? Who decides who is wrong? What do you do about followers who won't do anything unless they are told, who won't think for themselves? If any of these issues seem important to the group, try to bring other relevant scriptures into your discussion.

For both church leaders and members, 1 Peter 5:6-7 gives the foundation for risking humility. If you suspect you have trouble casting everything on God, you might explore what makes it difficult for you to do this. For instance, some people have bad experiences with their fathers and then never feel safe trusting God, elders, or other authorities.

As you discuss humble leadership and humble submission, look for ways to practice both in your group. Try not to be self-consciously "humble" when you pray together (Matthew 6:5), but you might take the opportunity to risk sounding foolish (humiliating yourself) in humbling yourselves before God in prayer.

Lesson twelve is very short, so you could continue at your next meeting anything you don't finish at this one.

114

Early Church Leadership

The New Testament gives no clear picture of how churches were organized. From scattered references we can make only a probable sketch.

A group of believers met periodically in the home of a member wealthy enough to have a spacious house (Romans 16:5). We call such a group a "house-church." A church (Greek: *ekklesia*; literally, "assembly") probably prayed, sang, and heard Scripture read and discussed (Colossians 3:16). They also ate together, celebrated the Lord's Supper, and baptized (1 Corinthians 1:13-17, 11:17-34). Poor members, widows, and orphans were cared for (1 Timothy 5:3-16). The doctrines of the faith were taught.

Leadership was probably modeled on the system Jewish synagogues used. A board of respected men called elders (Hebrew: *sanhedrin*; Greek: *gerousia*) oversaw the synagogues in a locality. Also, each synagogue was more or less run by the most respected men in the assembly. Likewise, a Christian house-church probably had several elders (1 Peter 5:1; Greek: *presbuteroi*) who worked both in committee and on divided responsibilities. These men administered discipline, settled friction among church members, saw to members' personal needs, and managed finances. *Deacons, overseers (bishops), pastors,* and *teachers* are named as local church officials in Romans 12:6-8, Ephesians 4:11, and 1 Timothy 3:1-13, but we do not know whether these titles denote different ranks or are just various terms for elders.[3]

Besides these local leaders, the Church also recognized some offices of leaders who were not attached to particular house-churches. *Apostles* had the highest authority. *Prophets* (1 Corinthians 12:38, Ephesians 4:11) were sometimes attached to a particular church (Acts 13:1), but at other times traveled from city to city with messages from the Lord (Acts 11:27-30). The *Didache*, a manual for churches from about 70-110 AD, records rules for discerning true prophets and regulating the hospitality such travelers might expect.[4] *Evangelists* and some *teachers* (Ephesians 4:11) also probably traveled.

115

1. Kelly, page 200.
2. Kelly, page 206.
3. Chadwick, pages 45-49.
4. The *Didache* is available in paperback in *Early Christian Writings,* edited by Maxwell Staniforth (New York: Penguin Books, 1968), pages 225-237.

1 PETER 5:8-14

Final Exhortations

If this short lesson doesn't give you enough to meditate on and discuss, you could return to any teachings on submission, humility, or suffering that you were not able to fully absorb before. Or, you could move ahead to the review in lesson thirteen.

For Further Study:
See other tactics for resisting the Devil in Ephesians 6:11-18. How can you put these into practice?

1. Casting all your anxieties on God (5:7) doesn't allow you to be lazy. While you are not worrying about your own needs, what does Peter want you to do instead (verse 8)?

_____

_____

_____

_____

_____

2. According to verses 8-9, how can we resist the Devil's attempts to devour us? Explain in your own words.

_____

_____

_____

_____

_____

117

3. a. As you strive to resist, you should focus on
   some facts about God and you (see 1:13).
   What future has "the God of all grace"
   planned for you (5:10)?

   _____

   _____

   _____

   _____

   b. In the meantime, what four things should
   you trust that God will do for you (verse 10)?
   Explain each in your own words.

   restore (NASB: perfect) _____

   _____

   _____

   _____

   make . . . strong (NASB: confirm) _____

   _____

   _____

   _____

   make . . . firm (NASB: strengthen) _____

   _____

   _____

   _____

   make . . . steadfast (NASB: establish) _____

   _____

   _____

   _____

4. In 2:13-5:11, Peter moves back and forth from
   discussing authority and submission (2:13-18,
   3:1-12, 5:1-7) to explaining how to respond to

118

trials and suffering (2:19-25, 3:13-4:19, 5:8-11). How are these two subjects—submission and response to trials—related?

_____

_____

_____

_____

_____

For Further Study:
Finish your outline of 1 Peter, if you are working on one. You might try a broad outline of the whole book now, or a detailed outline of a piece such as 4:12-5:11, if you have not experimented with outlining before.

5. How would you summarize Peter's message in 5:8-11?

_____

_____

_____

_____

_____

6. What insight from 5:8-11 most encourages you in your current situation?

_____

_____

_____

_____

_____

7. Is there anything you might do to apply some command or promise in 5:8-11 to the situations you are now facing? If so, write down how you might act in obedience, or how you might help let this truth sink into your heart.

_____

_____

_____

**Optional
Application:** How
might you help your
church or study group
to better reflect the
relationships you de-
scribed in question 8?

With the help of Silas (verse 12). Literally, "by Silvanus." "Silas" and "Silvanus" were Greek and
Latin versions of the same name. Silas was an
important leader in the early Church. He was a
prophet (Acts 15:32), a fellow missionary with
Paul (Acts 15:40), and an official emissary from
Jerusalem to the Antiochene church (Acts
15:22). With Paul, Silas co-authored 1 and
2 Thessalonians (1 Thessalonians 1:1, 2 Thessalonians 1:1).
     It is not clear what "by" Silvanus means.
He may have taken Peter's dictation, or had
some participation in drafting the letter.[1]

8. What do you learn about the early Church from
   the words "brother" (verse 12), "son" (verse 13),
   and "kiss of love" (verse 14)?

She who is in Babylon, chosen together with you
(verse 13). As John did in 2 John 1 and 13,
Peter referred to his local church as an 'elect
lady.' Christians conceived of the Church as
female, the Bride of Christ.
     As for "Babylon," Jews and Christians
often called Rome by this name, for what
Babylon was to the Old Testament prophets—
"the proud, immoral, godless city which domi-

nated" the world[2]—Rome was to Jews and
Christians of the first century AD. Ancient
sources record that Peter spent the last years of
his life in Rome.[3] Further, as 1 Peter 1:2 empha-
sizes, all Christians are "in Babylon" in that all
are in exile from their promised land. For these
reasons, many scholars believe that "she who is
in Babylon" means the church at Rome,
although some believe that "she" is the church,
or even Peter's wife, in the literal Babylon in
Mesopotamia.[4]

Mark (verse 13). John Mark had often visited Peter
when both had belonged to the Jerusalem
church (Acts 12:12-18). He had traveled with
Paul in the 40's (Acts 12:25, 13:13, 15:36-39),
and visited Paul in Rome around 60 AD (Colossians 4:10, Philemon 24, 2 Timothy 4:11). Tradi-
tion has it that in those later years Mark worked
with Peter in Rome, and that most of what
Mark wrote in his Gospel was Peter's teaching.[5]

9. List any questions you have about 5:8-14.

_____

_____

_____

_____

1. On this debate, see Kelly, pages 214-216; Stibbs, pages 25-30;
   Wuest, page 132.
2. Kelly, pages 218-220.
3. Among these ancient sources are Clement of Rome, Ignatius of
   Antioch, and Dionysius of Corinth; see Bruce, pages 402-410.
4. Stibbs; page 176, Kelly, page 208; see also Jensen, page 14,
   and Wuest's dissent in Wuest, pages 132-133.
5. Kelly, page 220; Stibbs, page 177; Jensen, page 75.

REVIEW

1. Reread all of 1 Peter. It should be familiar to you by now, so you should be able to read rapidly, looking for threads that tie the book together. Pray for a fresh perspective on what God is saying through this book.

   Also, review lesson one of this study, as well as any outlines or charts you made of 1 Peter. You might also look at the end of each lesson in this study for summaries you made for each passage. This may sound like a lot of work, but it will help you make connections among things you've learned and commit important truths to memory. But don't get bogged down and frustrated; do what you can with the time and skills God has given you.

Study Skill—Returning to the Purpose
Many teachers of Bible study stress the importance of returning to the author's purpose after detailed study of a book. J. I. Packer calls this the "spiral" approach to Bible study. *Our* purpose for studying the book may not be the same as the author's or first reader's, but their goals should affect how we interpret and apply what they say.

---

2. In lesson one, question 7, you said tentatively what you thought the main theme or purpose of this letter was. After closer study, how would you now summarize Peter's apparent main goal?

(To help you, you might review your summaries of each passage on pages 32, 44, 55, 61, 87, 94-95, 99, 105, and 119.)

_____

_____

_____

_____

_____

_____

3. Most students think 1 Peter divides into three parts after the address—1:3-2:10, 2:11-4:11, and 4:12-5:12. (See page 56 for an alternate view.) You may find that just summarizing these three main sections will help you see the book as a whole. So, write down a sentence or title that you think explains the point of each passage.

1:1-2 _Address: The Christian's Identity_

1:3-2:10 _____

_____

_____

_____

2:11-4:11 _____

_____

_____

_____

4:12-5:12 _____

_____

_____

5:13-14 _Closing_____

124

4. What were the most important lessons you learned from your study of 1 Peter on the following topics?

Suffering _____

_____

_____

_____

_____

_____

Authority and submission _____

_____

_____

_____

_____

_____

_____

Doing good _____

_____

_____

_____

_____

Relationships with other people _____

_____

_____

_____

_____

_____

Your identity in Christ _____

_____

_____

_____

_____

Other _____

_____

_____

_____

_____

_____

Study Skill—Keeping Lists
A list like the one described on page 30 can help you recall what you learned on a given topic.

5. One of the main topics of the letter is what God has done to and for us through Christ. Summarize what Peter has to say in the following passages about who we are.

1:3-9 _____

_____

_____

_____

_____

_____

2:4-9 _____

_____

_____

_____

_____

_____

6. In each of the following verses, Peter describes a kind of abuse his readers experienced. For each verse, name the *kind of abuse*. Then tell how Peter wanted Christians to *respond*, and explain what *aim or belief should motivate* a Christian to act in that way.

2:12

kind of abuse
proper response
motive

3:9

kind of abuse
proper response
motive

3:16

kind of abuse
proper response
motive

4:4

kind of abuse
proper response
motive

4:14-16

kind of abuse
proper response
motive

7. Look back at the questions you listed at the end of lessons one through twelve. Do any questions that seem important to you remain unanswered? If so, some of the sources on pages 133-137 may help you to answer those questions. Or, you might study some particular passage with cross-references on your own.

For Further Study:
Some people prefer to outline a book after thoroughly studying all of it. If you decided not to outline 1 Peter as you went along, you might like to try outlining it now. For help in outlining, see pages 15-16, 18, and 56.

8. Have you noticed any areas (thoughts, attitudes, opinions, behavior) in which you have changed as a result of studying 1 Peter? If so, explain how you have changed.

_____

_____

_____

_____

_____

_____

_____

9. Look back over the entire study at questions in which you expressed a desire to make some specific application. Are you satisfied with your follow-through? Pray about any of those areas that you think you should continue to pursue specifically. (Now that you have completed this study, perhaps something new has come to mind that you would like to concentrate on. If so, bring it before God in prayer as well.) Write any notes here.

_____

_____

_____

_____

_____

_____

_____

For the group

You might organize your discussion around three questions: 1) What have you learned from your study of 1 Peter; 2) How have you changed as a result of your study; and 3) Where will you go from here? You may be more able to see each other's growth than your own. Think about why change has or has not occurred. Try to encourage each other without expecting instant results.

Give everyone a chance to ask questions he or she still has about the book. See if you can plan how to answer them.

Then, evaluate how well your group functioned during your study of 1 Peter. (You might take a whole meeting for this.) Some questions you might ask are:

> What did you learn about small group study?
> How well did the study help you grasp the book of 1 Peter?
> What were the most important truths you discovered together about the Lord?
> What did you like best about your meetings? What did you like least? What would you change?
> How well did you meet the goals you set at your first meeting?
> What are members' current needs? What will you do next?

GOING ON IN 1 PETER

The Christ Peter Knew

For Peter, the necessity of Christ's suffering (1 Peter 1:11) was no dry doctrine, but a lesson learned through his own bitter errors and the agony of his dearest friend. To understand more fully what the gospel of the suffering Messiah meant to Peter, consider studying one or more of the events of his time with Jesus.

Walking on Water. *Matthew 14:22-33* recounts events of the evening after Jesus fed five thousand men and their families on five loaves and two fish. Notice how Peter responded on first and second thought to Jesus' invitation to walk with Him on the water. Think also about what the disciples believed their confession of verse 33 meant in light of their experiences that night and the previous day. Did Jesus appear to have been sent to suffer? (Key words: *faith, salvation, Son of God.*)

Peter's Confession. *Matthew 16:13-28* records more of Peter's pre-Resurrection understanding of Jesus' identity and mission. What did he expect the Christ to be and do? How did he react to the notion that the Christ must suffer? Why did he react so? What reasons did Jesus give for why He and His disciples had to suffer?

The Transfiguration. *Matthew 17:1-8* follows six days after Peter's confession in 16:13-28. What does Peter's reaction to the Transfiguration tell you about his understanding of the Christ?

The Foot-washing. *John 13:1-15* tells what happened when Jesus washed His disciples' feet at the Last Supper. Notice how Peter reacted to the gesture, and why. What did he show about his view of Jesus' role? Reflect on what Jesus meant the gesture to teach about His own and His followers' missions. What did Peter misunderstand?

The Arrest. *John 18:10-13* describes what Peter did when the soldiers came to arrest Jesus. Why do you think he acted like this? What understand-

131

ing of the Christ did he show? How do you think he felt when Jesus healed the wounded slave (*Luke 22:50-51*) and then let Himself be arrested?

Peter's Denial. *John 13:36-38* shows that Peter and Jesus assessed differently Peter's loyalty to Jesus. *John 18:15-18,25-27* proves Jesus right. Why do you suppose Peter was so confident at supper? Why did he deny Jesus hours later? Do you think he was committed to the real Christ, or to a false notion of Him? Think about how Peter might have felt about how Jesus responded to His arrest.

Do You Love Me? *John 21:15-23* tells how Jesus reinstated Peter as the apostles' leader after Peter's denial and Jesus' resurrection. Why do you think Jesus asked three times if Peter loved Him? How did Peter feel to be asked three times? What do you think Jesus' threefold command means, and implies about love? What light does this scene shed on Peter's letter to Asia Minor?

STUDY AIDS

For further information on the material covered in this study, you might consider the following sources. If your local bookstore does not have them, you can have the bookstore order them from the publisher, or you can find them in most seminary libraries. Many university and public libraries will also carry these books.

Commentaries on 1 Peter

Kelly, J. N. D. *A Commentary on the Epistles of Peter and Jude* (Baker, 1969).
Thorough, verse-by-verse commentary from a conservative point of view. Kelly is very readable for ordinary people, and not wearyingly long. For those who want to know all the nuances of a Greek word or the Jewish background to something Peter says, Kelly includes these in parentheses. However, Kelly's scholarship should not get in a reader's way.

Stibbs, Alan M. *The First Epistle General of Peter* (Eerdmans, 1959).
Like Kelly, Stibbs mainly gives exegesis (explanation of the text) rather than exposition (preaching and application). Stibbs is even briefer and less technical than Kelly.

Wuest, Kenneth. *First Peter in the Greek New Testament* (Eerdmans, 1942).
Wuest chooses key Greek words from most verses to explain for people who know no Greek. He brings out the richness of each word with clear definitions and illustrations. Eerdmans reprints this material in *Word Studies in the Greek New Testament* by Wuest.

Baxter, J. Sidlow. *Explore the Book* (Zondervan, 1960).
This was originally a six-volume survey course of the whole Bible, but it became so popular that Zondervan has printed it in one 1800-page volume since 1966. Baxter does not give verse-by-verse commentary, but

instead gives clear broad outlines, overviews of each book, and review questions. Each chapter of Baxter's work is a "lesson" that assigns a portion of Scripture to be read and then gives enough exposition, commentary, and practical application to orient the reader. Baxter was a great preacher, and his style is inspiring. The lesson on 1 Peter is excellent for pulling the book together.

Historical Sources

Bruce, F. F. *New Testament History* (Doubleday, 1979).
> A readable history of Herodian kings, Roman governors, philosophical schools, Jewish sects, Jesus, the early Jerusalem church, Paul, and early gentile Christianity. Well documented with footnotes for the serious student, but the notes do not intrude.

Harrison, E. F. *Introduction to the New Testament* (Eerdmans, 1971).
> History from Alexander the Great—who made Greek culture dominant in the biblical world—through philosophies, pagan and Jewish religion, Jesus' ministry and teaching (the weakest section), and the spread of Christianity. Very good maps and photographs of the land, art, and architecture of New Testament times.

Concordances, Dictionaries, and Handbooks

A *concordance* lists words of the Bible alphabetically along with each verse in which the word appears. It lets you do your own word studies. An *exhaustive* concordance lists every word used in a given translation, while an *abridged* or *complete* concordance omits either some words, some occurrences of the word, or both.

The two best exhaustive concordances are *Strong's Exhaustive Concordance* and *Young's Analytical Concordance to the Bible*. Both are based on the King James Version of the Bible. *Strong's* has an index by which you can find out which Greek or Hebrew word is used in a given English verse. *Young's* breaks up each English word it translates. However, neither concordance requires knowledge of the original language.

Among other good, less expensive concordances, *Cruden's Complete Concordance* is keyed to the King James and Revised Versions, and *The NIV Complete Concordance* is keyed to the New International Version. These include all references to every word included, but they omit "minor" words. They also lack indexes to the original languages.

A *Bible dictionary* or *Bible encyclopedia* alphabetically lists articles about people, places, doctrines, important words, customs, and geography of the Bible.

The New Bible Dictionary, edited by J.D. Douglas, F.F. Bruce, J.I. Packer, N. Hillyer, D. Gutherie, A.R. Millard, and D.J. Wiseman (Tyndale, 1982) is more comprehensive than most dictionaries. Its 1300 pages include quantities of information along with excellent maps, charts, diagrams, and an index for cross-referencing.

Unger's Bible Dictionary by Merrill F. Unger (Moody, 1979) is equally excellent and is available in an inexpensive paperback edition.

The Zondervan Pictorial Encyclopedia edited by Merrill C. Tenney (Zondervan, 1975, 1976) is excellent and exhaustive. It is being revised and updated in the 1980's. However, its five 1000-page volumes are a financial investment, so all but very serious students may prefer to use it at a library.

Unlike a Bible dictionary in the above sense, *Vine's Expository Dictionary of New Testament Words* by W.E. Vine (various publishers) alphabetically lists major words used in the King James Version and defines each New Testament Greek word that KJV translates with that English word. *Vine's* lists verse references where that Greek word appears, so that you can do your own cross-references and word studies without knowing any Greek.

A good **Bible atlas** can be a great aid to understanding what is going on in a book of the Bible and how geography affected events. Here are a few good choices.

The MacMillan Atlas by Yohanan Aharoni and Michael Avi-Yonah (MacMillan, 1968, 1977) contains 264 maps, 89 photos, and 12 graphics. The many maps of individual events portray battles, movements of people, and changing boundaries in detail.

The New Bible Atlas by J.J. Bimson and J.P. Kane (Tyndale, 1984) has 73 maps, 34 photos, and 34 graphics. Its evangelical perspective, concise and helpful text, and excellent research make it a very good choice, but its greatest strength is its outstanding graphics, such as cross-sections of the Dead Sea.

The Bible Mapbook by Simon Jenkins (Lion, 1984) is much shorter and less expensive than most other atlases, and so it is a good first taste of the usefulness of maps. It contains 91 simple maps, very little text, and 20 graphics. Some of the graphics are computer-generated and intriguing.

The Moody Atlas of Bible Lands by Barry J. Beitzel (Moody, 1984) is scholarly, very evangelical, and fully of theological text, indexes, and references. This admirable reference work will be too deep and costly for some, but Beitzel shows vividly how God prepared the land of Israel perfectly for the acts of salvation He was going to accomplish in it.

A **handbook** of bible customs can also be useful. Some good ones are *Today's Handbook of Bible Times and Customs* by William L. Coleman (Bethany, 1984) and the less detailed *Daily Life in Bible Times* (Nelson, 1982).

For Small Group Leaders

The Small Group Leader's Handbook by Steve Barker et al. (InterVarsity, 1982).

Written by an InterVarsity small group with college students primarily in mind. It includes information on small group dynamics and how to lead in light of them, and many ideas for worship, building community, and outreach. It has a good chapter on doing inductive Bible study

Getting Together: A Guide for Good Groups by Em Griffin (InterVarsity, 1982).
Applies to all kinds of groups, not just Bible studies. From his own experience, Griffin draws deep insights into why people join groups; how people relate to each other; and principles of leadership, decision making, and discussions. It is fun to read, but its 229 pages will take more time than the above book.

You Can Start a Bible Study Group by Gladys Hunt (Harold Shaw, 1984).
Builds on Hunt's thirty years of experience leading groups. This book is wonderfully focused on God's enabling. It is both clear and applicable for Bible study groups of all kinds.

How to Build a Small Groups Ministry by Neal F. McBride (NavPress, 1994).
This hands-on workbook for pastors and lay leaders includes everything you need to know to develop a plan that fits your unique church. Through basic principles, case studies, and worksheets, McBride leads you through twelve logical steps for organizing and administering a small groups ministry.

How to Lead Small Groups by Neal F. McBride (NavPress, 1990).
Covers leadership skills for all kinds of small groups—Bible study, fellowship, task, and support groups. Filled with step-by-step guidance and practical exercises to help you grasp the critical aspects of small group leadership and dynamics.

DJ Plus, a special section in *Discipleship Journal* (NavPress, bimonthly).
Unique. Three pages of this feature are packed with practical ideas for small groups. Writers discuss what they are currently doing as small group members and leaders. To subscribe, write to Subscription Services, Post Office Box 54470, Boulder, Colorado 80323-4470.

Bible Study Methods

Braga, James. *How to Study the Bible* (Multnomah, 1982).
Clear chapters on a variety of approaches to Bible study: synthetic, geographical, cultural, historical, doctrinal, practical, and so on. Designed to help the ordinary person without seminary training to use these approaches.

Fee, Gordon, and Douglas Stuart. *How to Read the Bible For All Its Worth* (Zondervan, 1982).
After explaining in general what interpretation (exegesis) and application (hermneneutics) are, Fee and Stuart offer chapters on interpreting and applying the different kinds of writing in the Bible: Epistles, Gospels, Old Testament Law, Old Testament narrative, the Prophets, Psalms, Wisdom, and Revelation. Fee and Stuart also suggest good commentaries on each biblical book. They write as evangelical scholars who personally recognize Scripture as God's Word for their daily lives.

Jensen, Irving L. *Independent Bible Study* (Moody, 1963), and *Enjoy Your Bible* (Moody, 1962).

The former is a comprehensive introduction to the inductive Bible study method, especially the use of synthetic charts. The latter is a simpler introduction to the subject.

Wald, Oletta. *The Joy of Discovery in Bible Study* (Augsburg, 1975).

Wald focuses on issues such as how to observe all that is in a text, how to ask questions of a text, how to use grammar and passage structure to see the writer's point, and so on. Very helpful on these subjects.

Titles in the
Lifechange series:

BIBLE STUDIES AND SMALL-GROUP MATERIALS FROM NAVPRESS

BIBLE STUDY SERIES
Design for Discipleship
Foundation for Christian Living
God in You
Learning to Love
The Life and Ministry of
    Jesus Christ
LifeChange
Love One Another
Pilgrimage Guides
Radical Relationships
Studies in Christian Living
Thinking Through Discipleship

TOPICAL BIBLE STUDIES
Becoming a Woman of Excellence
Becoming a Woman of Freedom
Becoming a Woman of Prayer
Becoming a Woman of Purpose
The Blessing Study Guide
Celebrating Life!
Growing in Christ
Growing Strong in God's Family
Homemaking
Husbands and Wives
Intimacy with God
Jesus Cares for Women
Jesus Changes Women
Lessons on Assurance
Lessons on Christian Living
Loving Your Husband
Loving Your Wife
A Mother's Legacy
Parents and Children
Praying from God's Heart
Strategies for a Successful
    Marriage
Surviving Life in the Fast Lane
To Run and Not Grow Tired
To Stand and Not Be Moved
To Walk and Not Grow Weary

What God Does When Men Pray
When the Squeeze is On

**BIBLE STUDIES WITH
COMPANION BOOKS**
Bold Love
Daughters of Eve
The Discipline of Grace
The Feminine Journey
From Bondage to Bonding
Hiding from Love
Inside Out
The Masculine Journey
The Practice of Godliness
The Pursuit of Holiness
Secret Longings of the Heart
Spiritual Disciplines for the
    Christian Life
Tame Your Fears
Transforming Grace
Trusting God
What Makes a Man?

SMALL-GROUP RESOURCES
201 Great Questions
Discipleship Journal's 101 Best
    Small-Group Ideas
How to Build a Small-Groups
    Ministry
How to Have Great Small-Group
    Meetings
How to Lead Small Groups
The Navigator Bible Studies
    Handbook
New Testament LessonMaker
The Small-Group Leaders
    Training Course

NAVPRESS ◖
BRINGING TRUTH TO LIFE
www.navpress.org

Get your copies today at your local Christian bookstore, or call
(800) 366-7788 and ask for offer **NPBS**.

GROWING THROUGH COMMUNITY

Developed by The Navigators, the FOUNDATIONS
FOR CHRISTIAN LIVING series is designed to help a
group become a small, closely knit community
motivated and empowered to worship
and serve God. Each study delves specifically
into an aspect of the faith that is essential to
becoming more like Christ. These powerful
studies offer rich insights and life-changing
truths that can move a believer beyond
knowledge about God to a personal,
rewarding experience in knowing God.

Paperback/$6 each
Christlikeness
Intimacy
Outreach
Relationships
Restoration
Warfare
Work
Worship

Get your copies today at your local bookstore,
or call (800) 366-7788 and ask for offer **#2014**.

NAVPRESS
BRINGING TRUTH TO LIFE
www.navpress.org

A NEW WAY TO STUDY
THE BIBLE

RADICAL RELATIONSHIPS is a conversational Bible study series that focuses on discovery and dialog—not fill-in-the-blank answers or a particular application. It's designed to help you dig into the New Testament, wrestle with what Jesus says, and raise the questions that are important to you. This series doesn't require preparation time and you don't need an expert leader. And each study can be tailored to a 30- or 60- minute format—whichever works best for you and your group!

Paperback/$7 each
Jesus' Farewell Teachings
Jesus on Relationships
The Uniqueness of Jesus

Get your copies today at your local bookstore, or call (800) 366-7788 and ask for offer **#2014**.